Monday Morning™

Language Arts Centers:
Riddles & Rhymes

by Claudia D. Vurnakes
Illustrated by
Marilynn G. Barr

Publisher: Roberta Suid
Copy Editor: Carol Whiteley
Design and Production: Marilynn G. Barr
Educational Consultant: Lillian Lieberman

Monday Morning Books is a trademark of
Monday Morning Books, Inc.

ISBN 1-878279-57-2

Printed in the United States of America

9 8 7 6 5 4 3 2 1

CONTENTS

INTRODUCTION

"My students really enjoy working at independent learning centers!"

"Learning centers are colorful, attractive, and add interest to the curriculum!"

"Manipulatives are helping me break out of the worksheet habit!"

Teachers all over are rediscovering the benefits of learning centers, which can challenge advanced students as well as help slower students brush up weak skill areas. But some teachers are worried that learning centers take a lot of time to create, or that artistic skills are required to make the centers appealing.

That's where this book comes in. *Riddles & Rhymes* provides all the patterns and activities you need to construct ten self-contained language-arts skills learning centers. Each of the centers features five different activities that focus on a particular skill, enabling the center to be used in a variety of ways. Activities are provided both for individual work and for cooperative learning. And you can decide whether to have children complete one activity a day, or work through an entire center at their own speed.

All the centers in *Riddles & Rhymes* are literature based, so you can incorporate them into larger units of study. The riddle and rhyme themes, such as "Where do you find hippopotamuses?" and "Little Miss Muffet," are favorites with children, and can be used to stimulate reading, creative writing, drama, art, even playground fun. Each center has a suggested grade level indicated, but choose the skills you want to work on according to the needs of your students.

While the centers can be used in a number of ways, they're easy to construct and don't require artistic talent or hard-to-find materials. Each center provides directions for arranging and working with the materials for each activity, and directions for constructing the learning center display panels are given here.

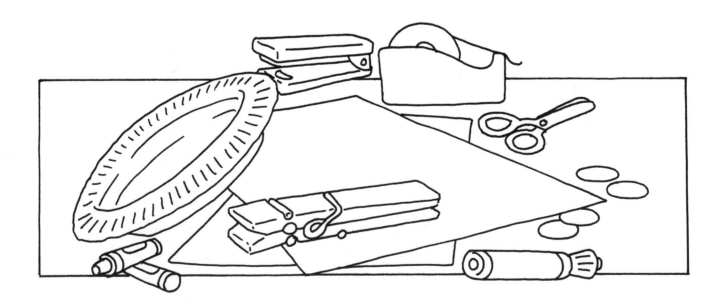

CONSTRUCTION TIPS

The learning centers described here are free-standing, folded panels. We recommend using three panels per center that measure approximately 19" x 24" each, but feel free to alter the dimensions to suit your classroom space and storage area.

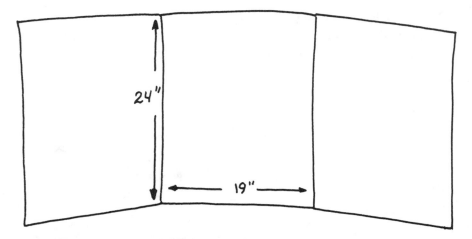

Use a stiff, strong material for your learning center panels—both corrugated cardboard and foam art board work well. You may want to glue bright paper to the panels or spray-paint them to provide colorful, eye-catching backgrounds. Small art pieces are provided in each chapter that you can color and glue to the panels for additional appeal.

Hinge the panels together with durable tape at least two inches wide; duct tape is great for this. Position the panels so that you have a quarter- to a half-inch gap between them. Then tape the fronts and backs to make hinges that will allow you to fold the panels flat for storage. You may also want to tape the outside edges of the center to prevent frayed corners. The time you spend constructing a durable center will really pay off.

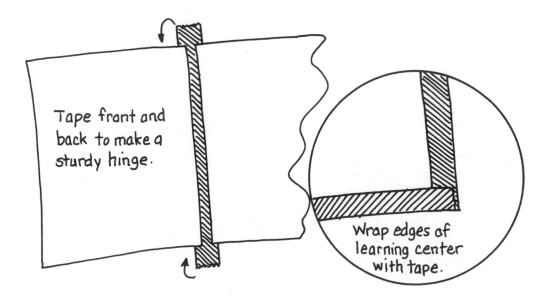

Tape front and back to make a sturdy hinge.

Wrap edges of learning center with tape.

ADDING SKILL PROGRAMMING

Duplicate the pages from this book for the learning center you want to make. Use markers, paint, or crayons to add color. Then cut out and glue the activities in position on your panels, using the illustration of the completed learning center at the front of the chapter as a guide.

For durable activity pieces and game boards, mount the pages on poster board and laminate before cutting them out. If you want to code the backs of pieces for self-checking, be sure to do that before you laminate.

STORING CENTER MATERIALS

Most of the activities are manipulative, so you need to plan how you will store the materials. For pockets glued or stapled directly on the panels, use paper plates cut in half, small flat boxes, manila envelopes, or library pocket cards. Some centers suggest other means of storing pieces, such as paper cups attached with clothespins to the center.

ADDITIONAL MATERIALS

All of the materials necessary, in addition to those duplicated from the book, are easy to obtain, such as paper clips, game markers, and pennies. A specific list of required materials is provided on the first page of each learning center chapter; in activity directions, alternative materials are suggested for any that may not be right at hand. For example, if you don't have a piece of magnetic tape on which children are asked to press paper-clipped number cards, you can simply have the children use pinch-style clothespins to attach the cards to the center.

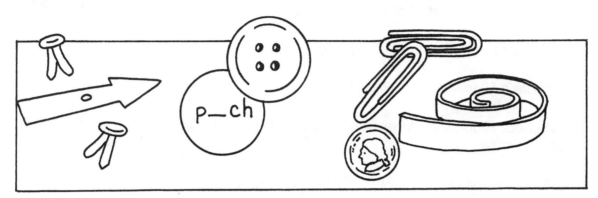

ADAPTING THE CENTERS TO OTHER SKILLS OR LEVELS

Many of the activities featured in *Riddles & Rhymes* can be easily adapted to other grade levels or used for different skills entirely. Just substitute your own student instruction boxes for the ones given here. Reprogram game cards and word wheels for the desired skill. You can extend the life of a learning center by clipping new instructions over old ones.

CENTERS WITH RIDDLE THEMES

Some of the centers in *Riddles & Rhymes* contain a riddle, for example, "Why do ducks fly upside down?" For first- and second-grade level centers, the answer to the riddle is placed behind a flap on the lower right-hand corner of the center. For third-grade level centers, the riddle answer is incorporated into one of the activities, giving students an extra challenge.

RESOURCE LIST

RIDDLES

The Carsick Zebra & Other Animal Riddles by David A. Adler (Holiday House, 1983).

Creepy, Crawly, Critter Riddles by Joanne Bernstein and Paul Cohen (Whitman, 1986).

Bennet Cerf's Book of Riddles by Bennet A. Cerf (Beginner Books, 1966).

World's Wackiest Riddle Book by Evelyn Jones (Sterling, 1987).

Old Turtle's Riddle & Joke Book by Leonard Kessler (Greenwillow, 1986).

Silly School Riddles & Other Classroom Crack-Ups by Caroline Levine (Whitman, 1984).

The Riddle Book by Roy McKie (Random House, 1978).

The Funniest Riddle Book Ever by Joseph Rosenbloom (Sterling, 1979).

Riddles & More Riddles by Michael J. Shannon (Children's Press, 1983).

RHYMES

The Mother Goose Treasury by Raymond Briggs (Dell, 1966).

Tomie de Paola's Mother Goose by Tomie de Paola (Putnam, 1985).

Marguerite De Angeli's Book of Nursery and Mother Goose Rhymes by Marguerite De Angeli (Doubleday, 1954).

The Random House Book of Mother Goose. A Treasury of 306 Timeless Nursery Rhymes by Arnold Lobel (Random House, 1986).

James Marshall's Mother Goose by James Marshall (Farrar, Straus & Giroux, 1986).

Richard Scarry's Best Mother Goose Ever by Richard Scarry (Golden, 1970).

Nursery Rhymes by Margaret Tarrant (Crowell, 1978).

Mother Goose by Tasha Tudor (Walck, 1972).

Jack and Jill

Materials:
Storage pockets, pinch clothespins,
four paper cups, poster board, glue,
two-inch brad, wipe-off crayons,
magnetic tape, paper clips.

Consonants

Jack and Jill
Went Up
the Hill

Jack and Jill

Jack and Jill

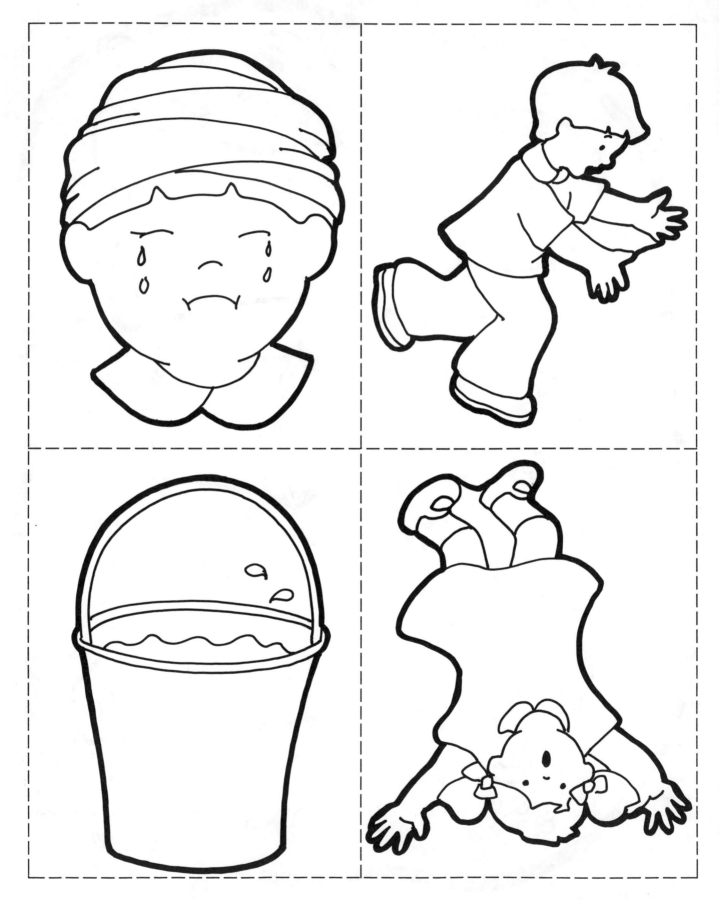

Jack and Jill

1. Take the picture cards from the pocket. Place each one in the correct bucket. Flip cards over to check.

Labels for paper cup buckets:

Jack

b

Jill

d

Note: Attach cups to learning center with pinch clothespins.

Note: Code backs of cards "b" or "d."

Jack and Jill

Note: Store cards in pocket on learning center.

Jack and Jill

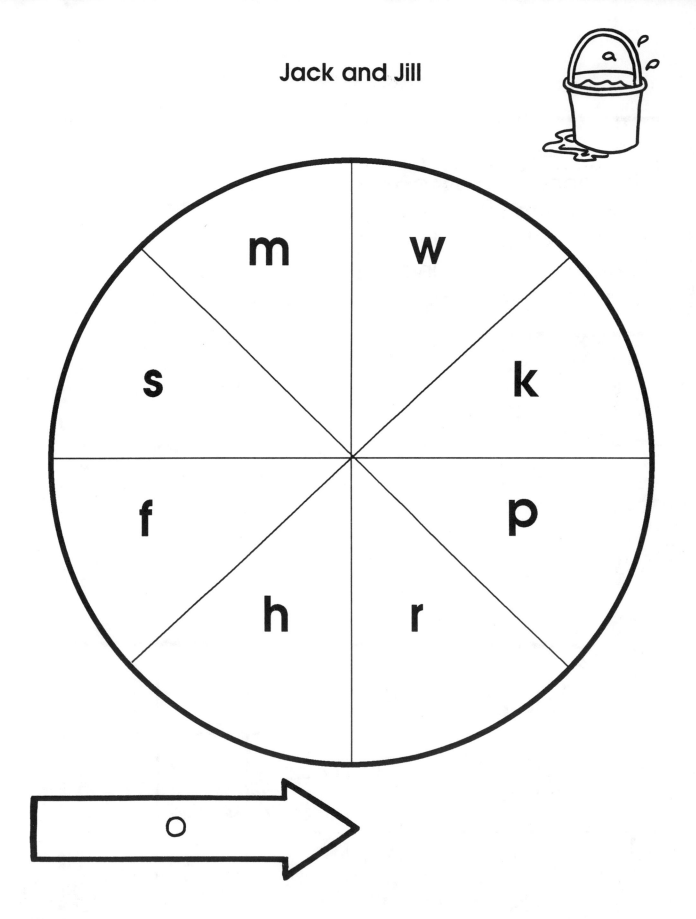

Note: Mount arrow on poster board and attach to wheel and center with two-inch brad.

3. Take the cards from the pocket. Draw a line through the pictures that begin with the same sound to make a tic-tac-toe.

Note: Store laminated tic-tac-toe cards in pocket on learning center. Provide a wipe-off crayon.

Jack and Jill

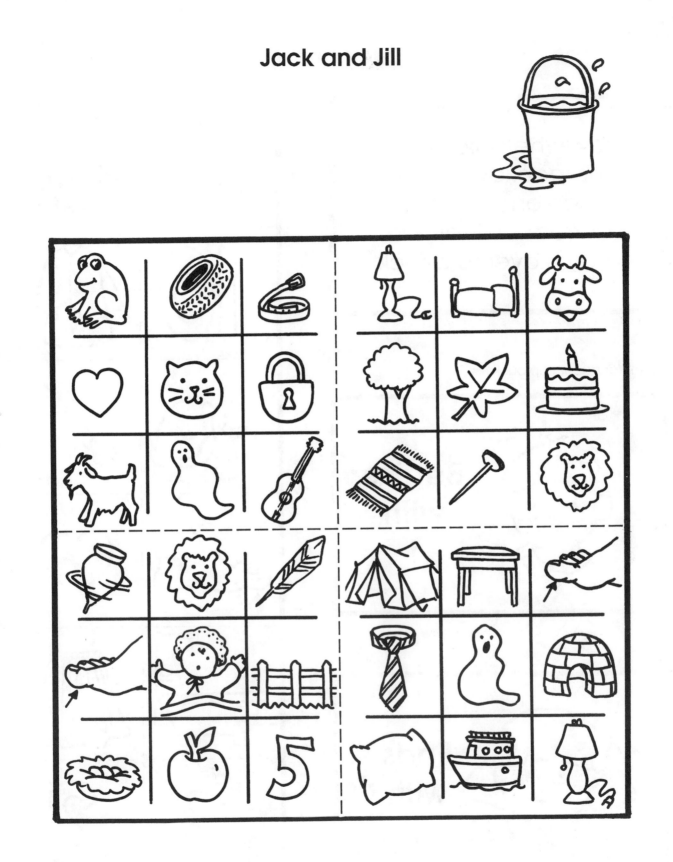

Jack and Jill

4. Take the cards from the pocket. Place each one in the correct bucket. Flip cards over to check.

Labels for paper cup buckets:

Begins with t

Ends with t

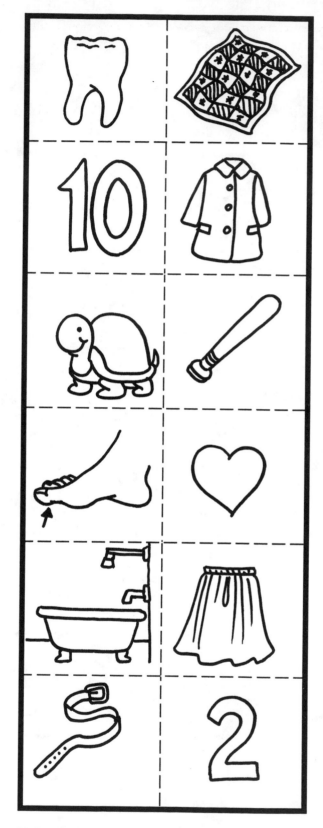

Note: Attach cups to learning center with pinch clothespins.

Note: Code backs of cards "begins" or "ends." Store cards in pocket on center.

Jack and Jill

5. Take the cards from the pocket. Place the correct cards on the well.

Note: Place paper clip on each card and store in pocket on center.

Jack and Jill

Note: To extend the activity, change the final consonant on the well to "d," "n," or "g."

Note: Place magnetic tape strips on dotted lines. Or attach cards to well with pinch clothespins.

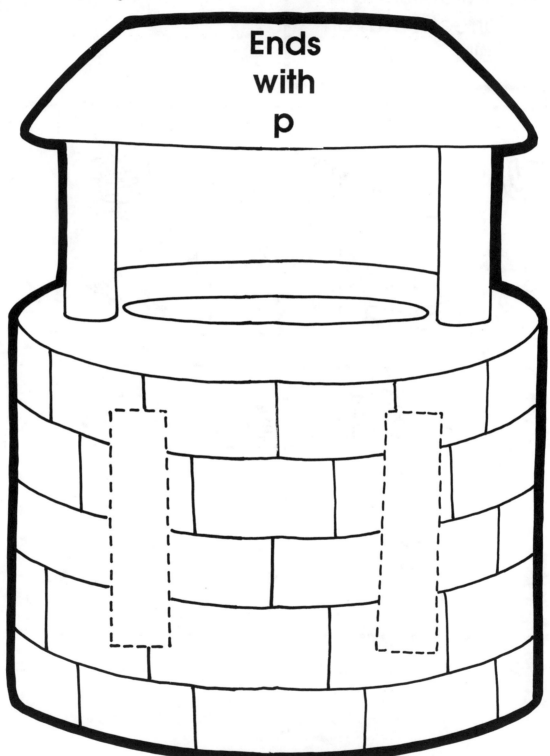

Ends
with
p

Why did the chicken cross the road?

Materials:
Storage pockets, egg carton, string,
poster board, glue, two-inch brad, tape,
hole punch, penny, game markers,
student paper.

Long and Short Vowels

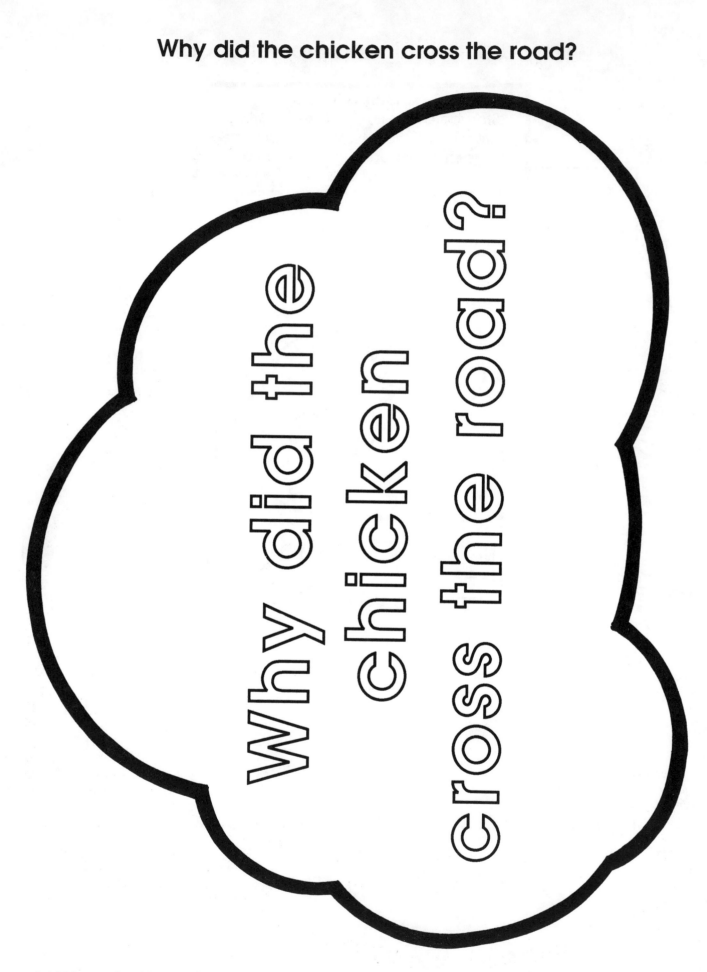

Why did the chicken cross the road?

23

Why did the chicken cross the road?

Why did the chicken cross the road?

1. Number your paper 1 to 20. Spin the spinner. Write a matching word from the list.

lace	fan	plane	cave
apple	flag	rain	lamp
hat	man	crab	baby
lake	gate	pail	snake
cap	ape	cake	bag
skate	hand	jam	paint

Why did the chicken cross the road?

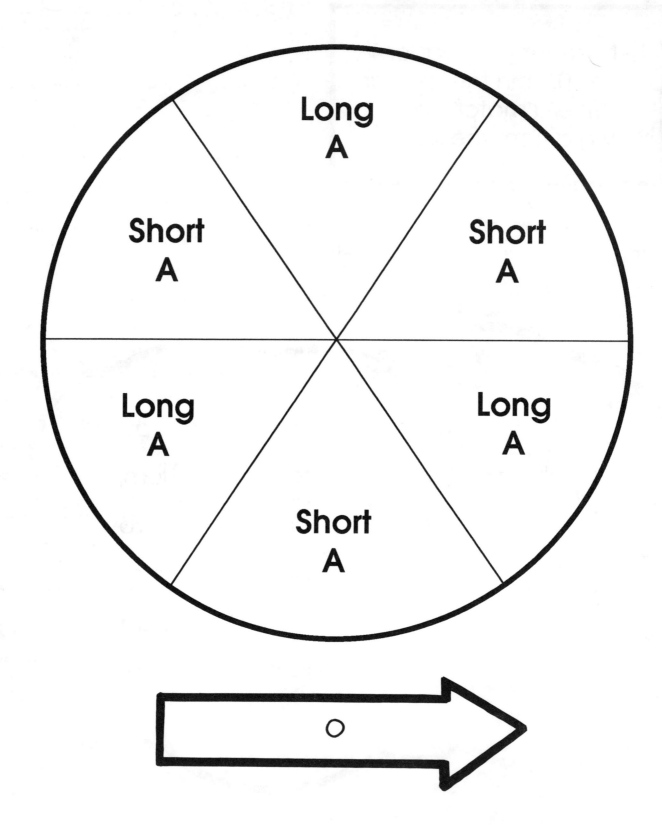

Note: Mount arrow on poster board.
Attach to wheel and center with two-inch brad.

26

Why did the chicken cross the road?

2. Short e's, please! Punch a hole next to each short e word.

Note: Students enjoy using a hole punch with this sheet. Use string to tie your punch to the center. The activity may also be completed by shading the correct circles. Duplicate the sheet and store copies in a pocket on the center.

○ bee	step	○
○ next	peach	○
○ seal	bed	○
○ cheese	leaf	○
○ sled	pen	○
○ fence	bell	○
○ leg	tree	○
○ eel	jet	○
○ tent	bean	○

Why did the chicken cross the road?

3. Put the long i words in the egg carton. Flip eggs over to check.

Note: Place an egg carton in front of the center for sorting.

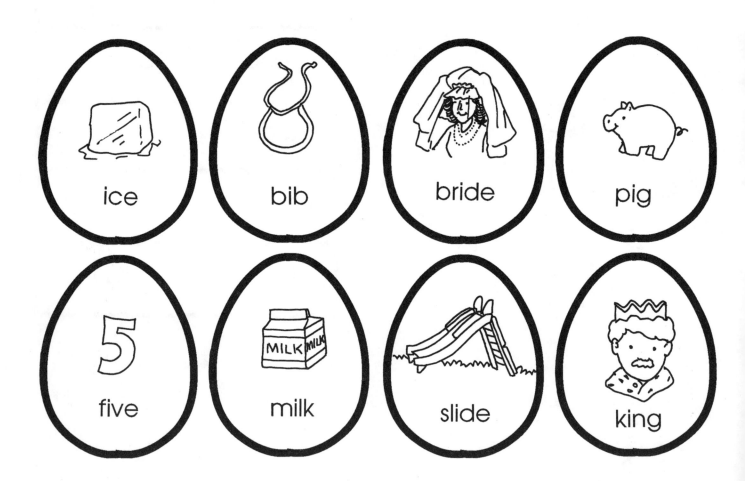

ice

bib

bride

pig

five

milk

slide

king

Why did the chicken cross the road?

ship

pipe

fish

fire

nine

kite

tire

spider

six

mice

crib

vine

Note: Code the backs of the eggs "L" and "S" for self-checking. Store in pocket on center.

Why did the chicken cross the road?

4. Game for Two Players

1. Take out the game board. Flip a penny. Heads = Move 1 space. Tails = Move 2 spaces.

2. Tell if the word you land on has a long or short u. Check the answer key.

3. If you are right, you stay. If you are wrong, you move back.

4. First to finish wins!

Answer Key

1. long	18. short
2. short	19. long
3. short	20. long
4. long	21. short
5. short	22. long
6. long	23. short
7. long	24. short
8. short	25. short
9. long	26. short
10. short	27. short
11. short	28. short
12. long	29. long
13. long	30. short
14. short	31. short
15. short	32. short
16. short	33. long
17. long	34. short

To get to the other side.

Note: To help students solve the learning center riddle, tape a flap in the lower right-hand corner. Under the flap, write this answer: "To get to the other side!"

Riddles & Rhymes

Why did the chicken cross the road?

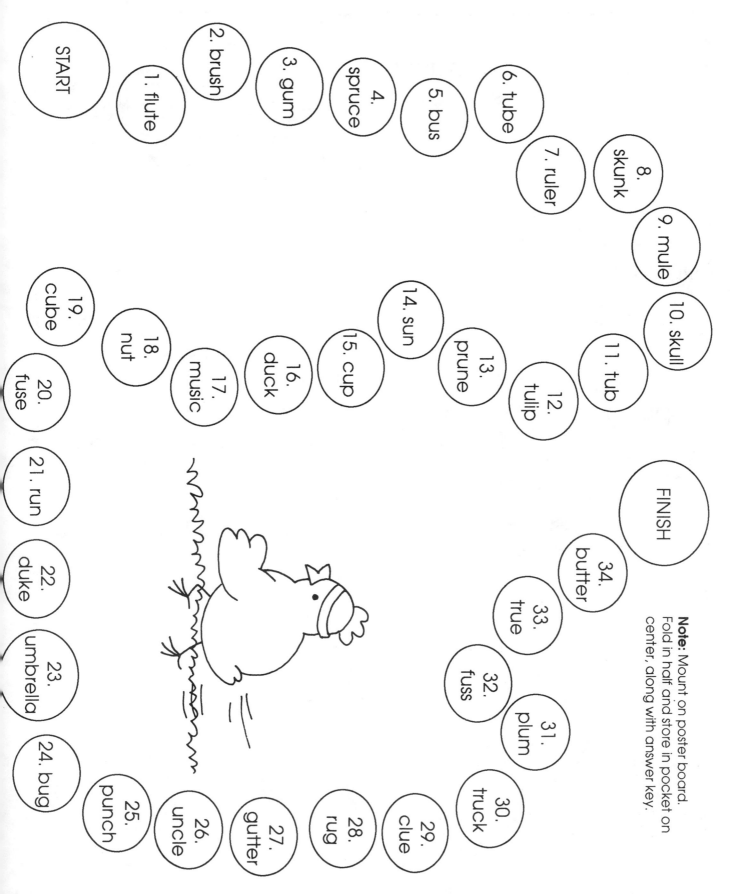

START

1. flute

2. brush

3. gum

4. spruce

5. bus

6. tube

7. ruler

8. skunk

9. mule

10. skull

11. tub

12. tulip

13. prune

14. sun

15. cup

16. duck

17. music

18. nut

19. cube

20. fuse

21. run

22. duke

23. umbrella

24. bug

25. punch

26. uncle

27. gutter

28. rug

29. clue

30. truck

31. plum

32. fuss

33. true

34. butter

FINISH

Note: Mount on poster board. Fold in half and store in pocket on center, along with answer key.

Why did the chicken cross the road?

5. Read the story. Write the short o words on your paper.

Fox and Hog sat on a log by a pond. Under the log was a box.

"Open the top," Hog said.

Fox chopped at the lock with a rock. The top popped open. Fox peeped inside. There was not one thing in the box. Then Fox put his hand in the box. He stopped.

"Feel!" he said. "This box is not empty. It has hot spots—lots! OUCH!"

Did you find 26 short o words?

The Three Little Kittens

Materials:
Storage pockets, wipe-off crayons,
aluminum pie pan, pinch clothespins,
wooden nickels (or circle cutouts),
sticky dots.

Punctuation

The Three Little Kittens Who Lost Their Mittens

Riddles & Rhymes

The Three Little Kittens

The Three Little Kittens

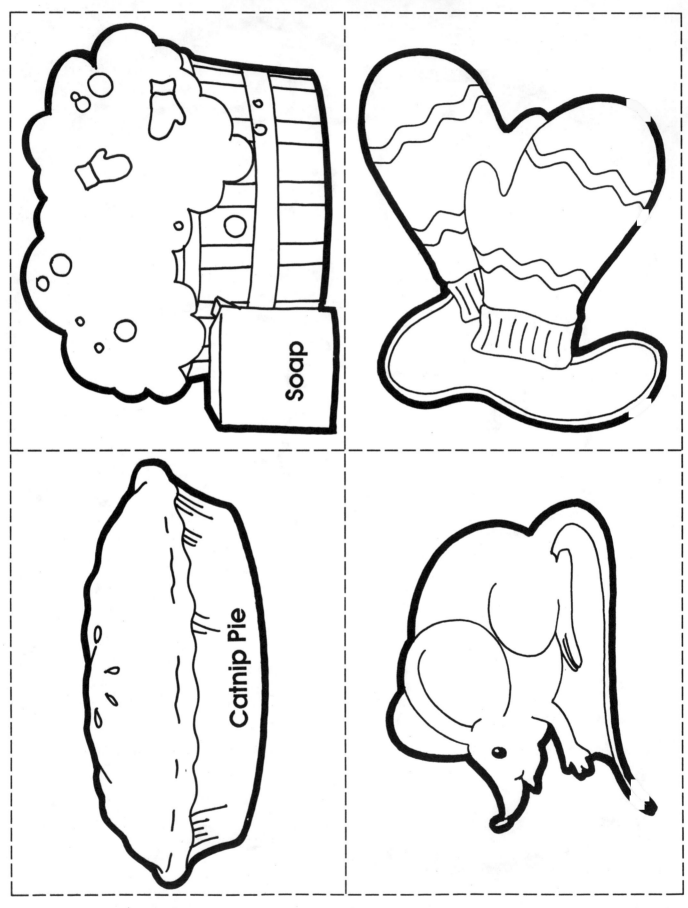

Soap

Catnip Pie

The Three Little Kittens

1. Find the telling sentences. Place them in the pie pan below. Flip the sentences to check.

The three little kittens _____	Hung them up to dry _____
The kittens lost their mittens _____	The kittens were _____
Cried and cried _____	Their mother made a pie _____
The mittens were dirty _____	She smelled a rat close by _____
They washed out their mittens _____	Good little kittens _____

Note: Provide an aluminum pie pan for sorting the correct activity pieces. If desired, laminate the sentence strips and provide a wipe-off crayon so students can write in the missing periods.

Note: Code the back of each sentence with a period. Store in pocket on center.

2. Find the asking sentences. Put them together. What do you see?

Note: Store puzzle pieces in pocket on center.

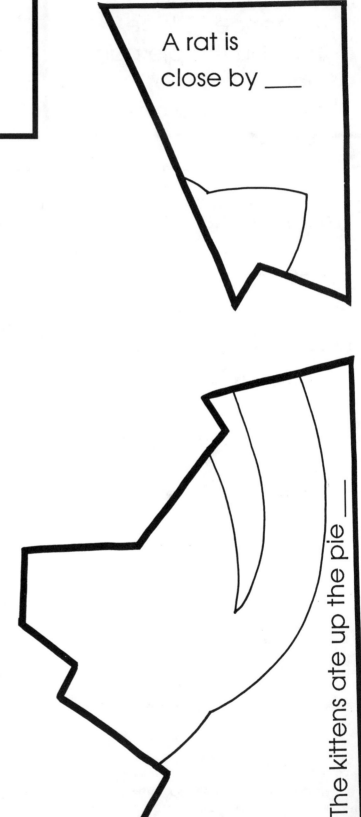

A rat is close by ___

The mittens are dirty ___

The kittens ate up the pie ___

The Three Little Kittens

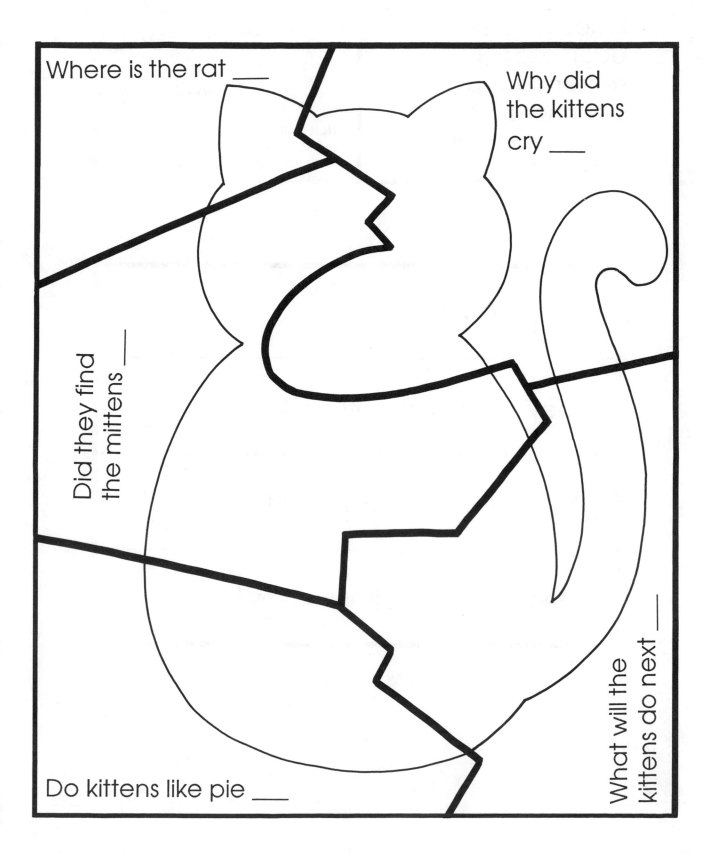

Where is the rat ___

Why did
the kittens
cry ___

Did they find
the mittens ___

Do kittens like pie ___

What will the
kittens do next ___

39

The Three Little Kittens

3. Place a (!) next to each exciting sentence. Flip the sentences over to check your answers.

Note: Label sticky dots with exclamation marks. Store in pocket with laminated sentence cards. For self-checking, code the backs with the correct punctuation mark.

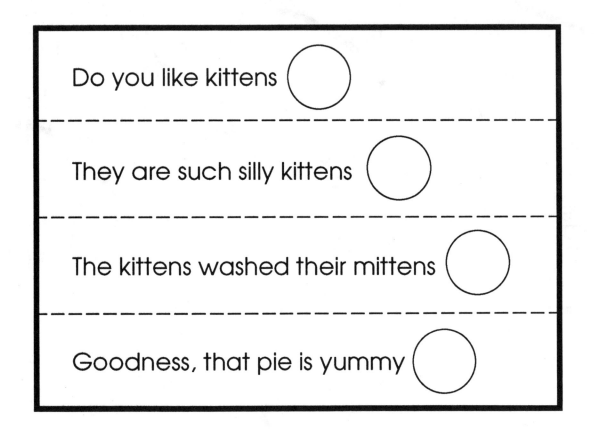

Do you like kittens ◯

They are such silly kittens ◯

The kittens washed their mittens ◯

Goodness, that pie is yummy ◯

The Three Little Kittens

The mittens were lost ◯

Wow, those mittens are very clean ◯

Where do kittens live ◯

Watch out — I see a rat ◯

Mama Cat just hates dirty mittens ◯

Most cats are clean animals ◯

Do dogs ever lick their paws ◯

Having a pet is terrific ◯

The Three Little Kittens

4. Clip each mitten card to the correct end mark.

Note: Label pinch clothespins with the three end marks. Clip to top of center. Store mitten cards in pocket on center.

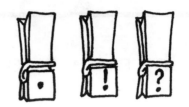

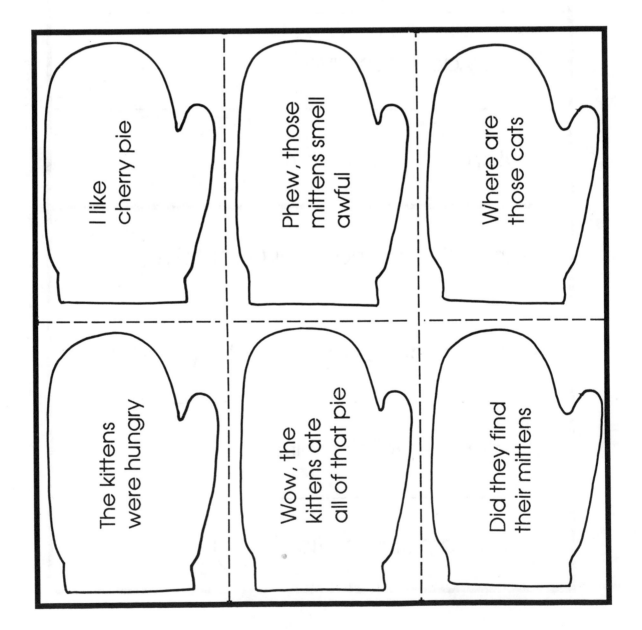

The Three Little Kittens

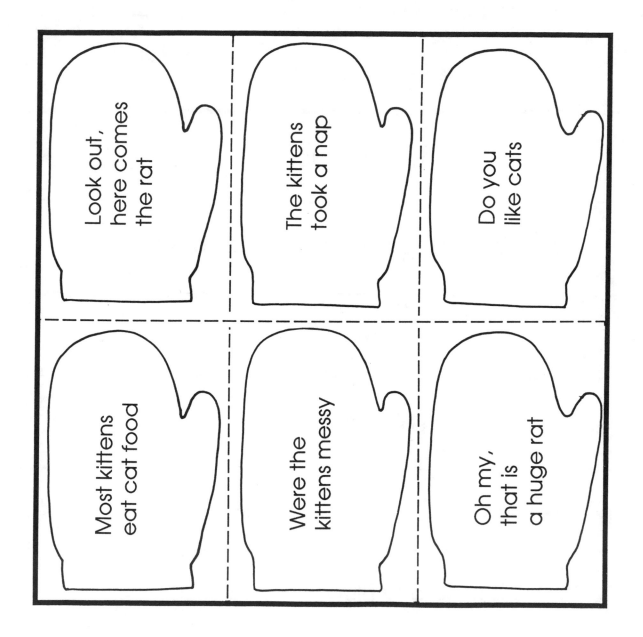

Look out,
here comes
the rat

The kittens
took a nap

Do you
like cats

Most kittens
eat cat food

Were the
kittens messy

Oh my,
that is
a huge rat

5. Place the correct end marker on each sentence card.

Note: Use with sentence strips that follow. Label eight wooden nickels with correct punctuation marks. Store in pocket on center with sentence strips.

The Three Little Kittens

The mouse ran up the clock

The black sheep had three bags of wool

The dish ran away with the spoon

Why did Georgie kiss the girls

Could the king's men fix Humpty

Where is Little Boy Blue

Oh my, Jack jumped over that candle

Wow, Mrs. Sprat ate everything

Why do firefighters wear red suspenders?

Materials:
Storage pockets, two paper cups,
pinch clothespins, poster board, glue,
two-inch brad, wipe-off crayon, tape,
two different-colored sets of 12 checkers, student paper.

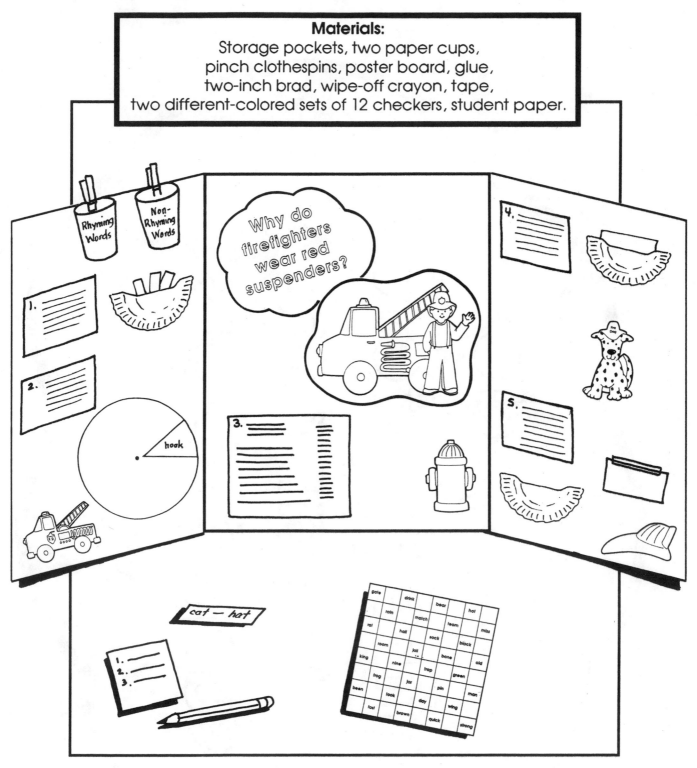

Rhyming Words

Why do firefighters wear red suspenders?

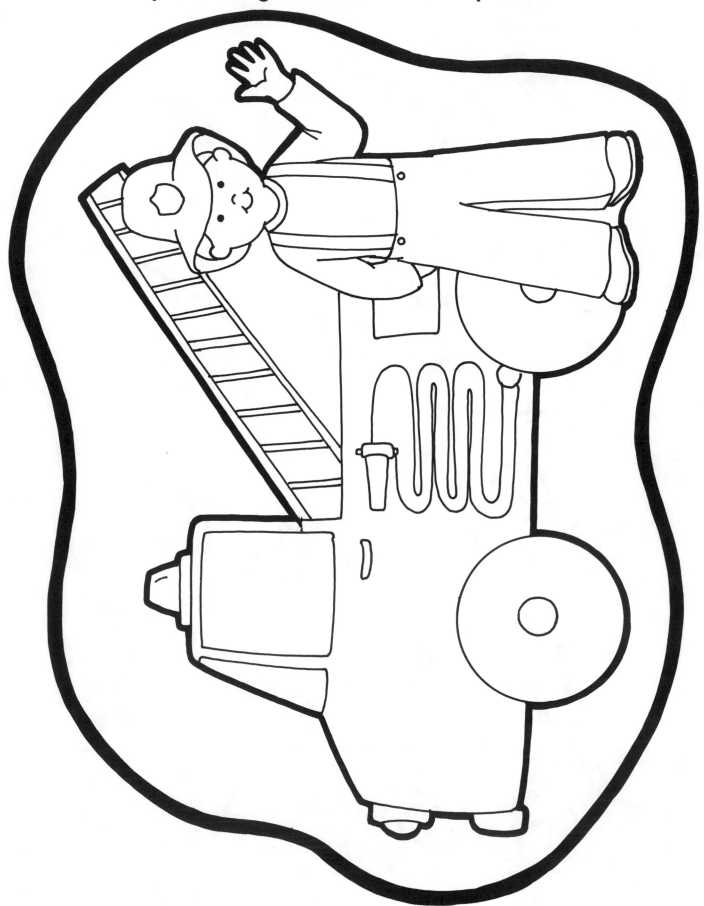

Why do firefighters wear red suspenders?

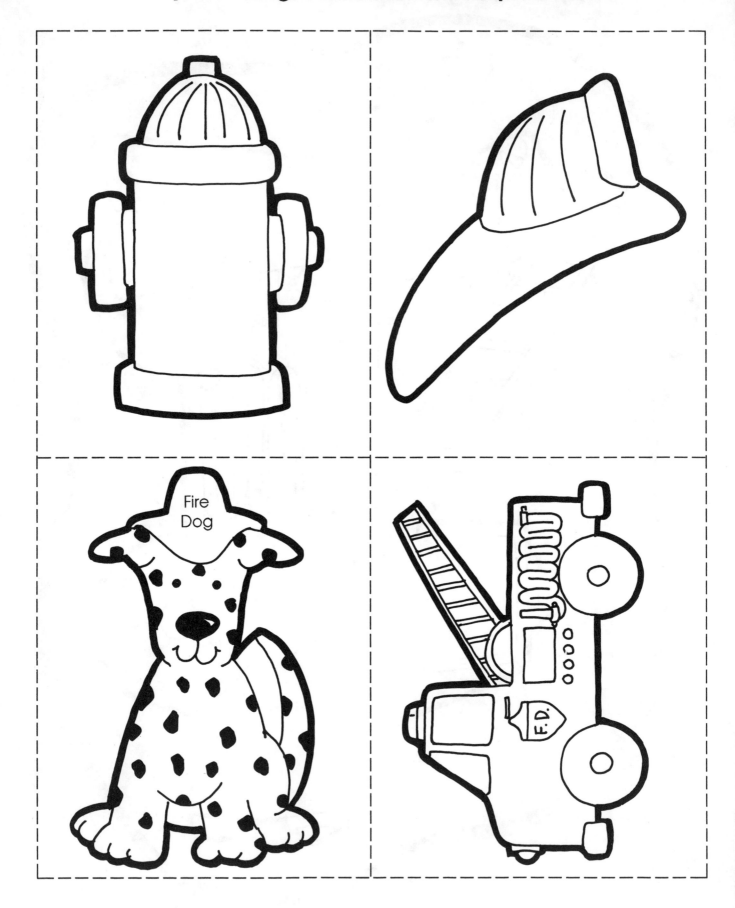

Fire
Dog

F.D.

48 Riddles & Rhymes

Why do firefighters wear red suspenders?

1. Take the cards from the pocket. Place each in the correct bucket. Flip cards over to check.

Labels for paper cup buckets:

Rhyming Words

Non-Rhyming Words

top - pot

pit - hit

had - red

car - star

doll - hot

hair - chair

saw - was

four - door

hand - hard

dice - mice

hat - tar

nose - rose

Note: Clip the cups to the learning center with pinch clothespins. Code the backs of the cards for self-checking.

Why do firefighters wear red suspenders?

2. Turn the dial. Read the word. Write three rhyming words on your own paper.

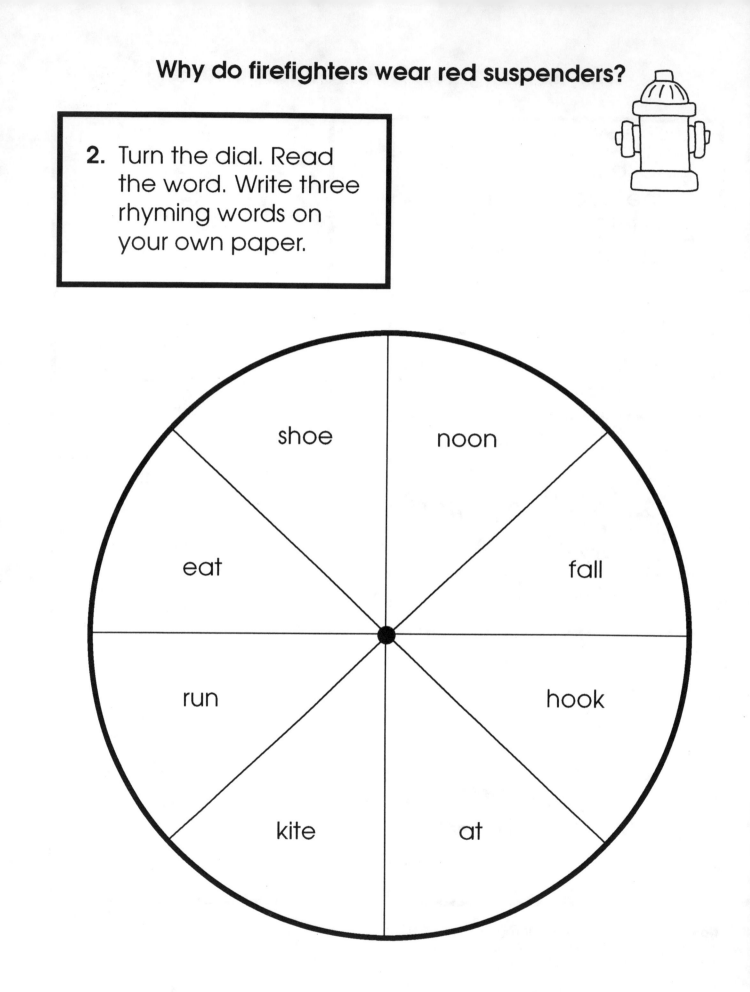

Why do firefighters wear red suspenders?

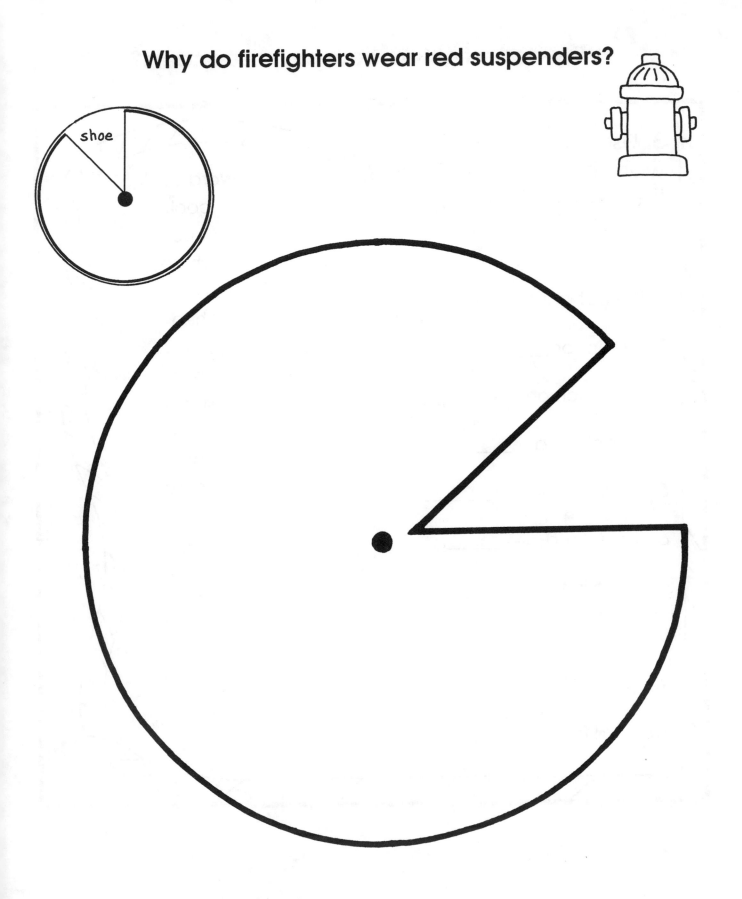

Note: Mount dial and dial cover on poster board and laminate. Attach to learning center with two-inch brad.

51

Why do firefighters wear red suspenders?

3. Use words from the word bank to finish these rhymes on your own paper.

1. the cat in the _____.

2. a mop for _____.

3. the spoon on the _____.

4. a book for a _____.

5. the mouse in the _____.

6. a pen for a _____.

7. a bee in the _____.

8. a bed on your _____.

9. a table for _____.

10. a tail for a _____.

Word Bank

cook
cup
whale
whip
hen
hand
hat
head
Mable
marble
house
hot
moon
men
Pop
tree
try

Why do firefighters wear red suspenders?

4. Use a wipe-off crayon to cross out the word on each line that does not rhyme.

Note: Laminate cards and store in pocket on center. Provide a wipe-off crayon.

big	wig	peg
third	toward	bird
colt	cold	gold
long	sting	song
ant	tent	cent
dry	fly	boy
dice	race	pace
love	have	dove
hand	friend	end
door	store	tar

Why do firefighters wear red suspenders?

five	live	have	lock	peg	dock
sang	wing	ring	flower	power	ever
six	tax	fix	lot	wet	pet
spot	hip	hot	rice	nice	race
tin	bone	stone	low	true	blow
go	snow	cow	leg	rag	bag
log	leg	hog	wheel	bell	steel
man	plan	time	mud	fun	flood
wish	fast	dish	belt	tall	wall
sing	pink	wink	gate	mad	late

Why do firefighters wear red suspenders?

5. Checkers Game for Two Players

1. Place your checkers on the board.

2. Take turns moving your checkers from square to square.

3. To keep your square, give a rhyming word.

Note: To help students solve the learning center riddle, tape a flap in the lower right-hand corner. Under the flap, write this answer: "To keep their pants up!"

Why do firefighters wear red suspenders?

Laminate and store folded in pocket on learning center.
Provide 12 checkers for each player.

gate		drink		bear		hot	
	rain		match		team		miss
rat		hall		sock		black	
	room		jail		bone		old
king		nine		trap		green	
	frog		jar		pin		man
been		took		day		wing	
	fast		brown		quick		strong

Little Boy Blue

Materials:
Storage pockets,
two paper cups,
wipe-off crayon,
penny, game markers.

Alphabetical Order

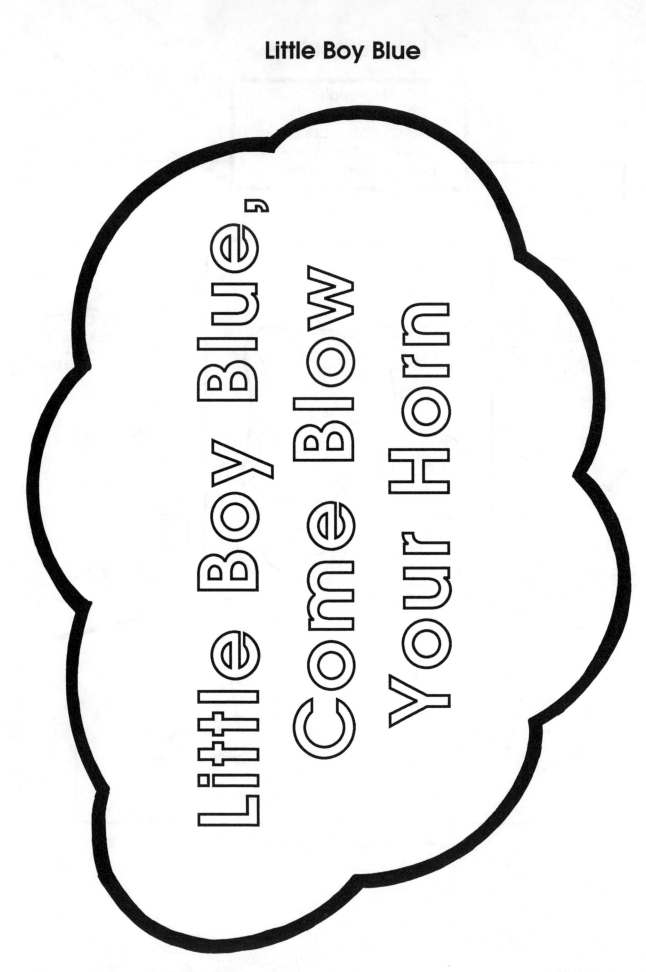

Little Boy Blue, Come Blow Your Horn

58

Riddles & Rhymes

Little Boy Blue

Little Boy Blue

Riddles & Rhymes

Little Boy Blue

1. Take the sheep cards from the pocket. Put them in ABC order. Flip the cards over to check.

Note: On the backs, number the cards in the correct alphabetical order. Store in pocket on center.

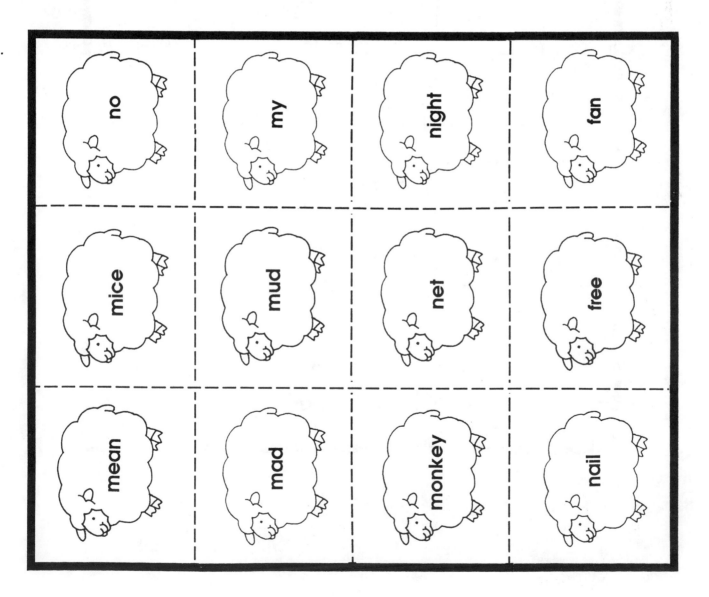

Little Boy Blue

2. Take the cards from the pocket. Put the cards that start with the same letter in ABC order.

Note: Store cards in pocket on center.

pepper	plate	boy	brave
end	even	jelly	judge
rose	rut	three	tick
tire	too	fat	fine

Little Boy Blue

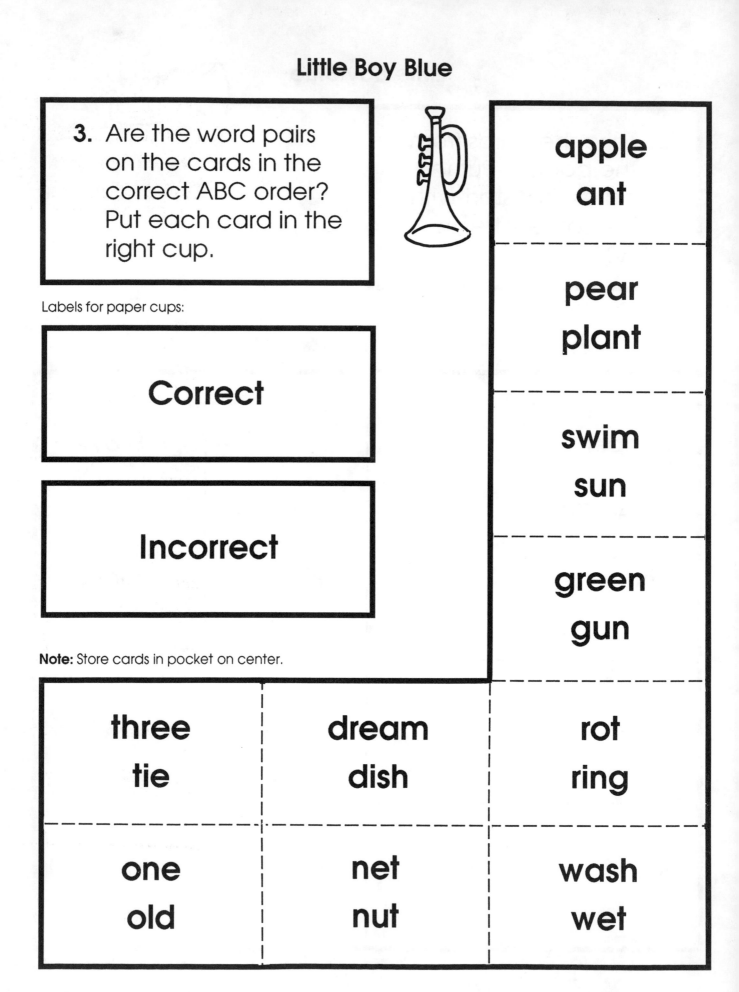

3. Are the word pairs on the cards in the correct ABC order? Put each card in the right cup.

Labels for paper cups:

Correct

Incorrect

Note: Store cards in pocket on center.

apple
ant

pear
plant

swim
sun

green
gun

three
tie

dream
dish

rot
ring

one
old

net
nut

wash
wet

4. Use a wipe-off crayon to number the words on each card in ABC order.

Note: Laminate cards and store in pocket on center. Provide a wipe-off crayon.

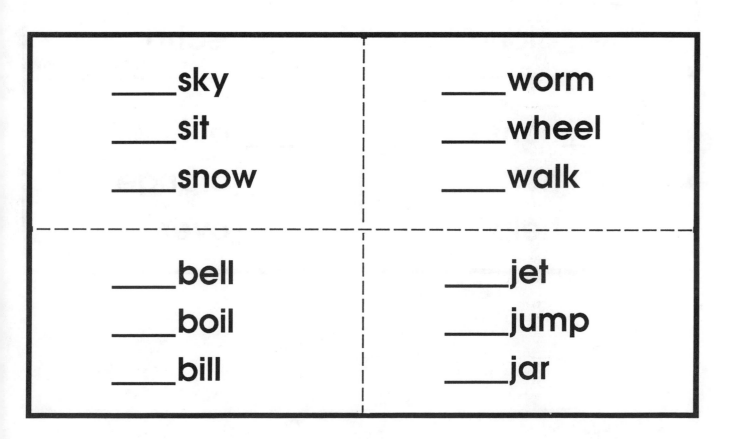

_____sky
_____sit
_____snow

_____worm
_____wheel
_____walk

_____bell
_____boil
_____bill

_____jet
_____jump
_____jar

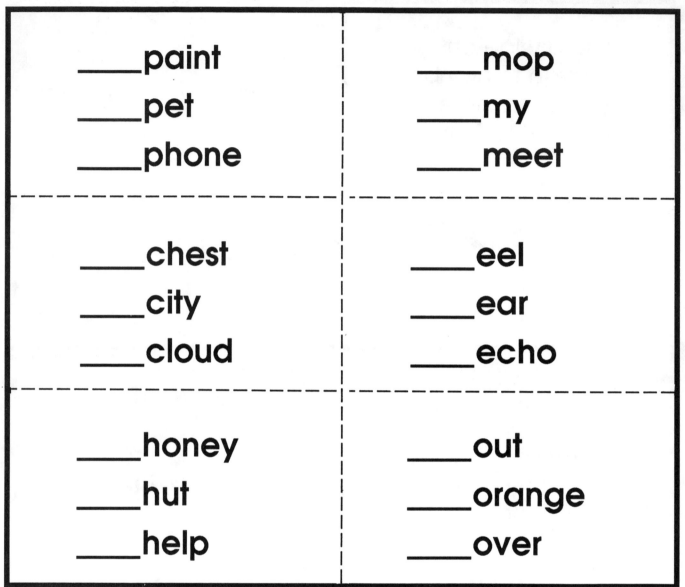

____paint

____pet

____phone

____mop

____my

____meet

____chest

____city

____cloud

____eel

____ear

____echo

____honey

____hut

____help

____out

____orange

____over

5. Game for Two Players

1. Take out the game board. Flip a penny.
   Heads = Move one space.
   Tails = Move two spaces.

2. Decide if the words you land on are in the correct ABC order. Check the answer key.

3. If you are right, keep your space. If you are wrong, move back.

4. First to finish wins!

Answer Key

1. incorrect	9. correct
2. correct	10. incorrect
3. correct	11. correct
4. incorrect	12. correct
5. correct	13. incorrect
6. incorrect	14. correct
7. incorrect	15. correct
8. incorrect	16. incorrect

Note: Store in pocket with game board.

Little Boy Blue

Laminate and fold in half to store in pocket, along with a penny and two game markers.

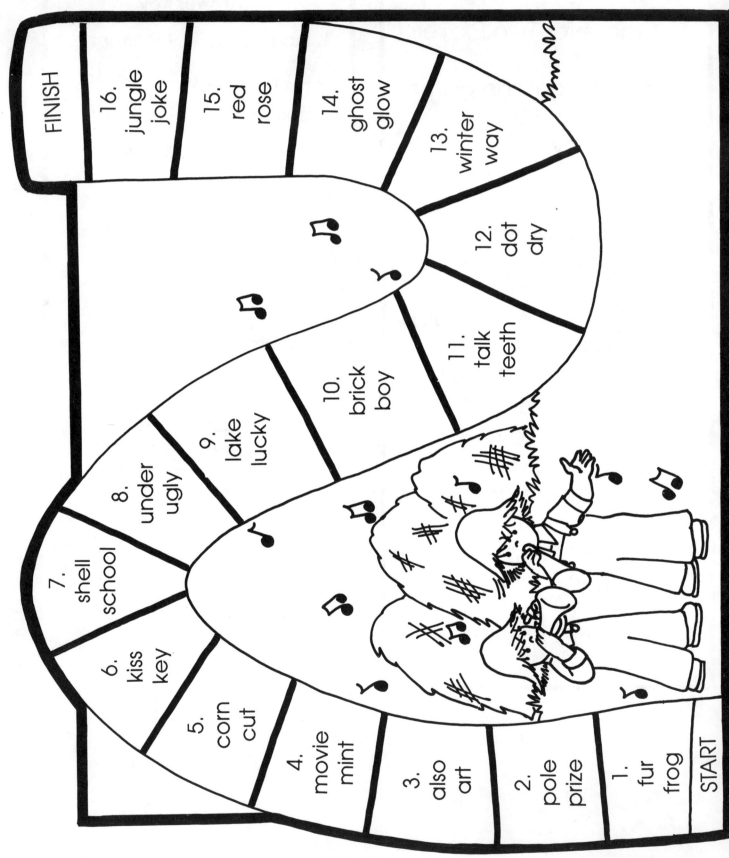

Riddles & Rhymes

Little Miss Muffet

Vowel Combinations

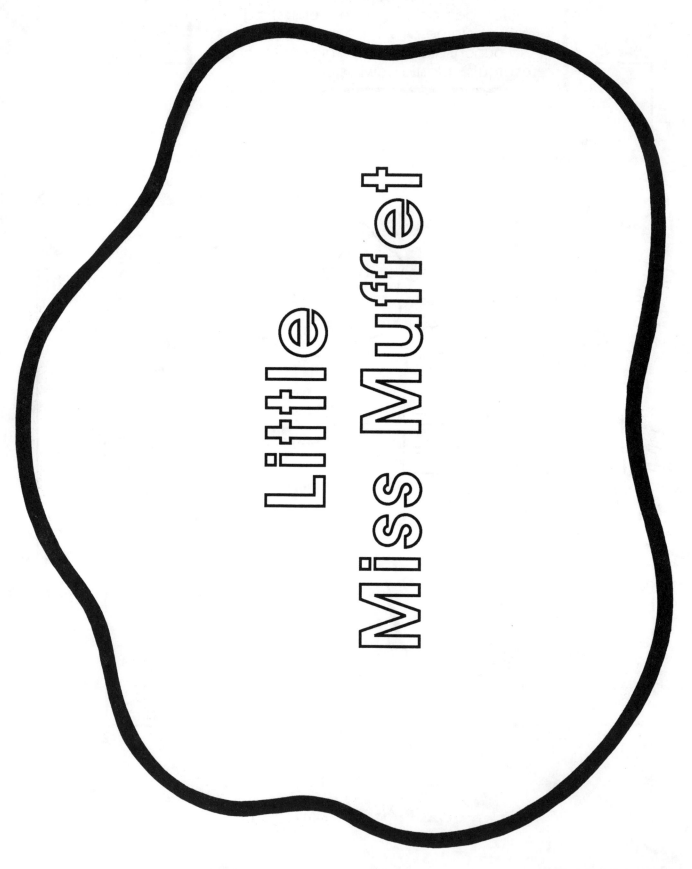

Little Miss Muffet

Little Miss Muffet

71

Little Miss Muffet

72
Riddles & Rhymes

Little Miss Muffet

1. Clip the clothespins to the correct spider.

Note: Clip paper cups to the learning center for clothespin storage. Store spider circles in pocket on center.

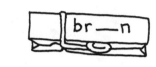

Label clothespins:

br ___ n   r ___ n
j ___ l   n ___ l
tr ___ l   p ___ d

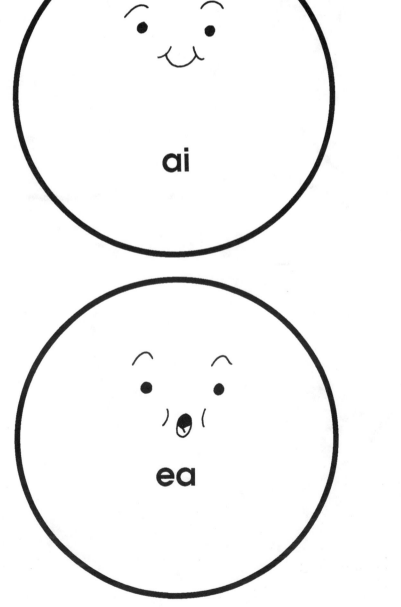

ai

ea

Label clothespins:

st ___ m   ___ gle
pl ___ se   t ___ m
n ___ t   scr ___ m

Little Miss Muffet

Label clothespins:

sh__p   j__p
str__t   ch__k
wh__l   s__d
qu__n

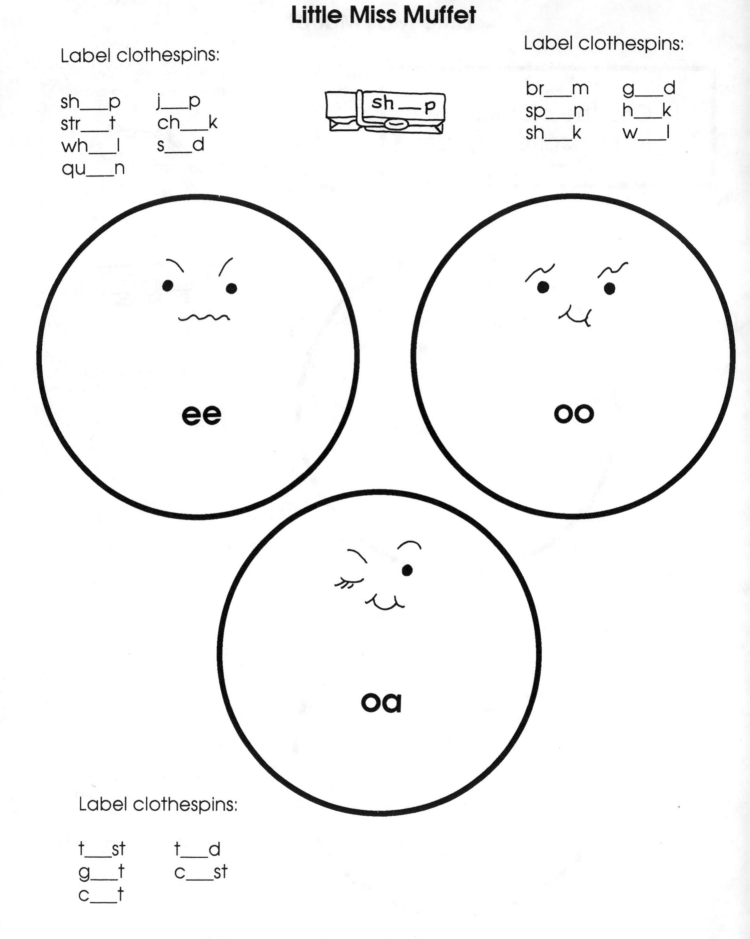

sh — p

Label clothespins:

br___m   g__d
sp__n   h__k
sh__k   w__l

ee

oo

oa

Label clothespins:

t__st   t__d
g__t   c__st
c__t

Little Miss Muffet

2. Use a hole punch to punch the correct vowels.

Note: Use string to tie a hole punch to the learning center. The activity may also be completed by coloring in the correct circles. Duplicate the punch sheet and store copies in a pocket on the center.

Punch the correct vowels.		
○ ee	p___nt	ai ○
○ ea	t___cher	ee ○
○ ow	b___t	oa ○
○ ee	tr___	ea ○
○ ee	___t	ea ○
○ ai	ch___n	ay ○
○ oa	b___k	oo ○
○ ay	r___d	ea ○
○ oa	sp___n	oo ○
○ ee	sp___d	ea ○
○ ai	pl___	ay ○

Little Miss Muffet

Punch the correct vowels.		
○ ai	sn___l	ee ○
○ oa	c___kie	oo ○
○ ee	s___d	ea ○
○ ai	h___t	ea ○
○ oa	s___p	oo ○
○ ee	thr___	ea ○
○ ee	r___n	ai ○
○ ea	b___ch	ai ○
○ oa	f___d	oo ○
○ ea	fr___ze	ee ○

Punch the correct vowels.		
○ oo	r___d	oa ○
○ ea	m___l	ee ○
○ oi	h___se	ou ○
○ oy	b___	ou ○
○ ay	tr___n	ai ○
○ ow	c___	ou ○
○ oo	r___f	oa ○
○ ou	cl___n	ow ○
○ ea	g___se	ee ○
○ ai	t___l	ee ○

Little Miss Muffet

3. Place the circles in the correct cereal bowls.

Note: Label wooden nickels or circle cutouts with words from the list below. Tape corresponding vowel combination labels on plastic bowls.

oi	ou	ow	oy
c___n	___t	___l	b___
n___se	h___se	t___n	j___
v___ce	m___se	fr___n	t___
j___n	s___r	cr___d	enj___
br___l	m___th	h___l	
		fl___er	

4. Roll-a-Cube
Roll the cube and use the word bank to make a word. Write it on your paper. Make ten words.

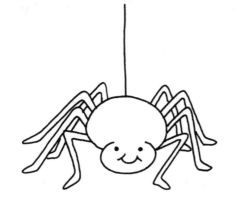

Word Bank

__l	f__t	p__l
b__t	f__d	pl__
b__ch	gr__	r__l
b__n	g__se	r__d
b__	g__t	s__
c__l	h__	sch__l
cl__	j__p	s__l
cr__n	l__f	s__p
ch__n	m__l	s__d
d__	m__t	sh__p
dr__n	n__l	t__m
__t	z__	tr__

78

Little Miss Muffet

Mount on poster board, laminate, and glue tabs to form a cube.

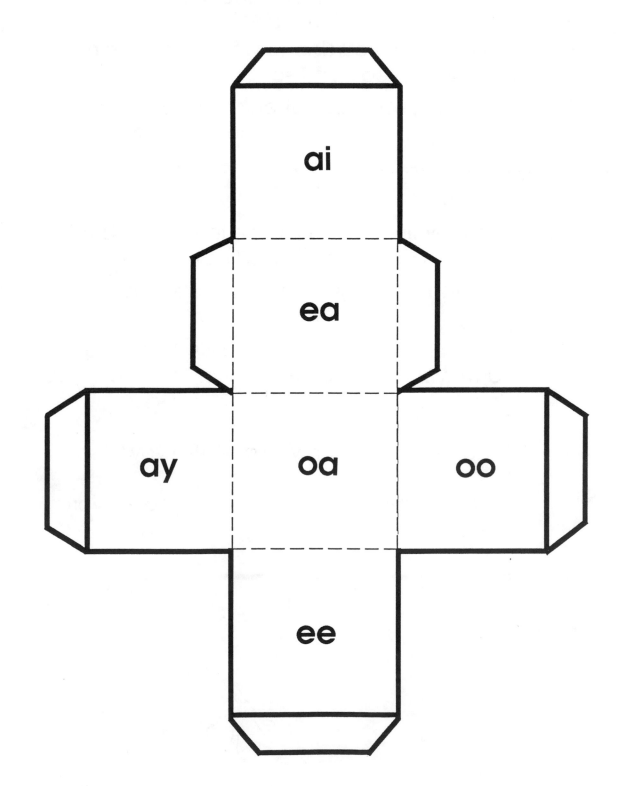

5. Read the story. Answer the questions.

"Oh, boy! I do enjoy curds and whey! They are my favorite choice for breakfast," said Miss Muffet.

She had just started to eat when she heard a loud noise. It was a big, ugly spider, the color of dirty oil.

The spider pointed at the curds.

"May I join you?" he asked.

After the spider finished eating, he left. Miss Muffet found some coins beside the soiled bowl.

"Oh, joy! Now I can buy a new toy!" she said.

1. On your paper, list all the words that have the same vowel sound you hear in "boil." Did you find 11?

2. What two ways can you spell the vowel sound?

3. Write a sentence of your own for each word you listed.

Old Mother Hubbard

Synonyms, Antonyms

Old Mother Hubbard

83

Old Mother Hubbard

Old Mother Hubbard

1. Put each bone with its correct synonym.

Labels for paper cups:

little

pretty

Note: To extend the activity, change cup labels and make new bones:

fast - quick, speedy, rapid, lively
hot - glowing, toasty, burning
quiet - silent, peaceful, still

big

85

Old Mother Hubbard

Note: Store cards in pocket on center.

small

huge

tiny

giant

short

enormous

miniature

gigantic

beautiful

handsome

cute

gorgeous

2. Rewrite this silly story on your own paper. For each underlined word, write a correct antonym.

One evening, Ms. Hubbard took a <u>short</u> walk in the woods. She <u>lost</u> an old puppy who was <u>strong</u> from hunger. She picked up the <u>huge</u> dog and took a <u>crooked</u> path home.

When Ms. Hubbard <u>closed</u> her cupboard, she discovered a <u>wonderful</u> problem. Her cupboard was <u>full</u>! Where could she get a <u>soft</u>, crunchy bone for her furry <u>enemy</u>? All the stores were <u>open</u> for the day.

Then Ms. Hubbard had an <u>awful</u> idea. She picked up the phone and ordered bones to <u>stop</u>!

Old Mother Hubbard

3. For each word on the list, spin the spinner. Write the synonym or antonym on your own paper.

Note: To extend the activity, make a new word list.

Word List

1. black	6. rich	11. cold
2. happy	7. all	12. scream
3. cold	8. late	13. top
4. fat	9. smile	14. begin
5. strong	10. brave	15. groan

Old Mother Hubbard

Mount arrow on poster board and attach to wheel with two-inch brad.

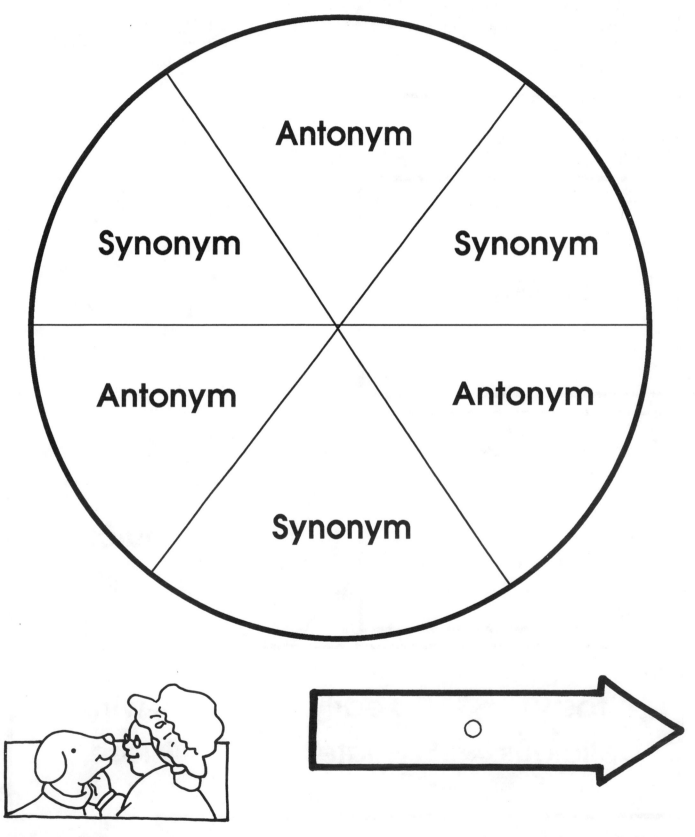

4. Place each word pair in the correct cup.

Labels for paper cups:

Antonyms

Synonyms

Note: Store cards in pocket on learning center.

quick
fast

| tasty delicious | early late | win lose |

Old Mother Hubbard

easy difficult	close near	off on
dry clean	city country	love adore
end finish	bag sack	wet damp
buy sell	baby infant	bright dim

Old Mother Hubbard

5. Old Mother Hubbard Game for Two Players

1. Shuffle the cards and deal them out.

2. In turn, choose a card from the other player.

3. Discard matching synonym and antonym pairs.

4. Don't be the player left holding the Old Mother Hubbard card!

Note: Label 24 game cards with the words below. Make a 25th card the Old Mother Hubbard card. Use artwork provided to decorate the backs of cards. Store cards in pocket on learning center.

center	strong	dirty
beach	loud	run
jog	yummy	middle
clean	front	shore
laugh	weak	tasty
night	noisy	giggle
rough	back	evening
money	cash	smooth

What happens when ducks fly upside down?

"R" Controlled Vowels

What happens when ducks fly upside down?

94

Riddles & Rhymes

What happens when ducks fly upside down?

What happens when ducks fly upside down?

What happens when ducks fly upside down?

1. Place each word card in the correct cup.

Labels for paper cups. Clip to center with clothespins.

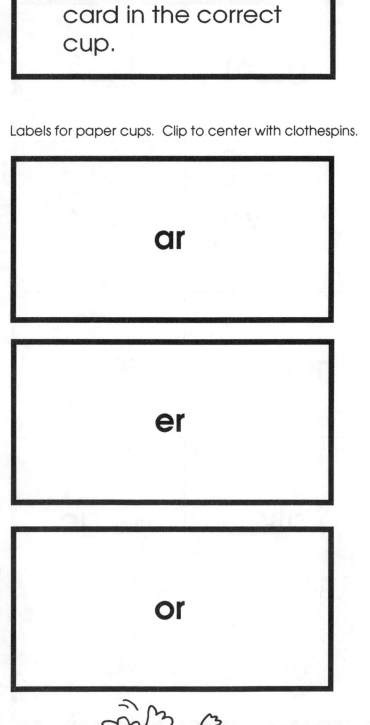

ar

er

or

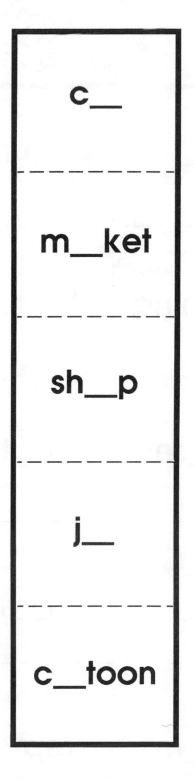

c__

m__ket

sh__p

j__

c__toon

Note: Store cards in pocket on center. Code backs if desired for self-checking.

What happens when ducks fly upside down?

c__n	p__fume	g__m	b__k
m__ning	t__mite	n__ve	c__t
h__se	t__t	hamm__	sm__t
h__n	n__th	silv__	l__ge
st__m	rep__t	wint__	d__t

Riddles & Rhymes

What happens when ducks fly upside down?

<table>
<tr><td>2.</td><td>Fill in the missing letters. Punch the correct words.</td></tr>
</table>

Note: Use string to tie your hole punch to the learning center. The activity may also be completed by coloring in the correct circles.

Note: Duplicate punch strips. Store in pocket on center.

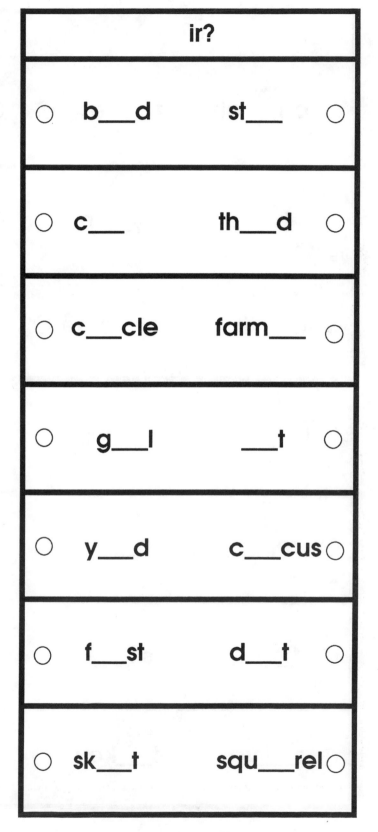

ir?

○ b__d   st__ ○

○ c__   th__d ○

○ c__cle   farm__ ○

○ g__l   __t ○

○ y__d   c__cus ○

○ f__st   d__t ○

○ sk__t   squ__rel ○

What happens when ducks fly upside down?

ur?			ar?		
○ ch___ch	t___tle ○		○ teach___	st___ ○	
○ b___n	y___n ○		○ p___ty	gl___y ○	
○ n___th	s___prise ○		○ d___t	f___m ○	
○ h___t	c___tain ○		○ g___l	h___p ○	
○ rep___t	n___se ○		○ c___pet	h___d ○	
○ f___	sk___t ○		○ ___m	s___f ○	
○ s___ve	t___key ○		○ sm___t	y___d ○	

Riddles & Rhymes

What happens when ducks fly upside down?

3. **Red Light, Green Light for Two Players**

   1. Pick a card. Tell what letters are missing.

   2. Your partner shows the green light if you are correct. He or she shows the red light if you are wrong.

Note: Store cards and stoplight in pocket on center. For additional drill, use cards from Activity 1.

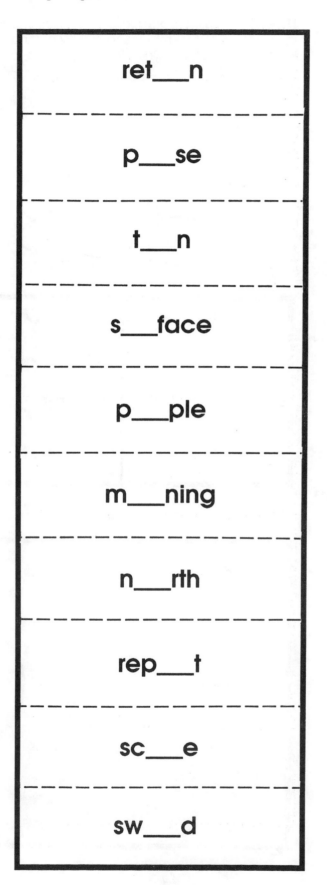

ret___n

p___se

t___n

s___face

p___ple

m___ning

n___rth

rep___t

sc___e

sw___d

What happens when ducks fly upside down?

Note: Color as indicated, mount on poster board, and laminate. Assemble stoplight by cutting as indicated and threading strip through slits so color shows in circle.

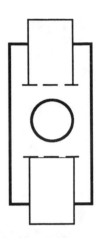

	Color green		Color red	

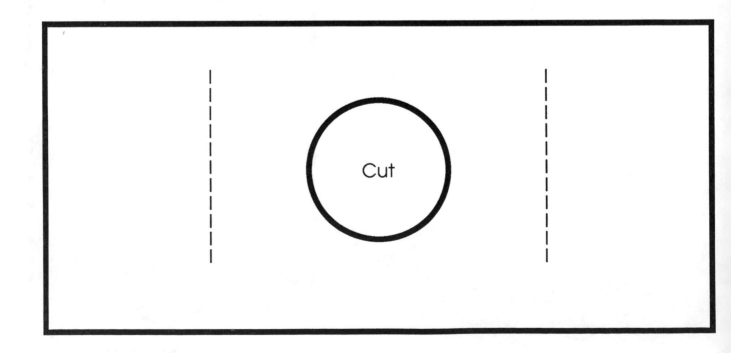

Cut

102   Riddles & Rhymes

What happens when ducks fly upside down?

4. Use a wipe-off crayon to fill in the blanks. Choose -ar, -er, -ir, -or, -ur.

M___tha and N___man drove their c___ to the p___k. It was a w___m wint___ aft___noon, p___fect for a picnic.

"What's for dinn___?" Norman asked. "S___dines? B___gers? P___k chops? I'm st___ved!"

Just then, th___ty ducks swam to the sh___e. They m___ched over to Martha and Norman. The noise was t___rible!

"Supp___ time!" shouted Martha. "It's soup and quack___s!"

Note: Laminate activity card. Provide a wipe-off marker.

What happens when ducks fly upside down?

5. Use a wipe-off crayon to circle the correctly spelled -ur words. Use the code letters to read the answer to the learning center riddle.

Note: Laminate activity card and store in pocket on center. Provide a wipe-off crayon.

1. hurd - K
   purple - T
   curn - P

2. turtle - H
   gurl - S
   urm - B

3. furst - O
   yurd - I
   nurse - E

4. curpet - W
   burn - Y
   thurd - V

5. curtain - Q
   lurge - C
   sture - G

6. murket - E
   purson - O
   turkey - U

7. murmaid - I
   fur - A
   snure - Y

8. wintur - S
   burd - M
   turn - C

9. hurry - K
   smurt - N
   repurt - D

10. sward - O
    curl - U
    turmite - A

11. purfume - L
    nurmal - F
    surprise - P

___ ___ ___ ___   ___ ___ ___ ___ ___   ___ ___
 1   2   3   4   5   6   7   8   9   10 11!

Where do you find hippopotamuses?

Materials:
Storage pockets, cup hooks, masking tape, scissors, two different-colored sets of 12 checkers, wipe-off crayons, poster board, glue, crayons, two-inch brad, buttons or Bingo-type chips.

Plurals

Where do you find hippopotamuses?

Where do you find hippopotamuses?

Riddles & Rhymes

Where do you find hippopotamuses?

Where do you find hippopotamuses?

Where do you find hippopotamuses?

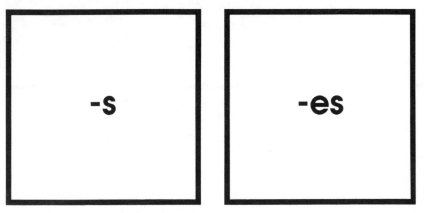

---

1. Hang each tag on the correct plural hook.

Note: To attach cup hooks to the center, poke a hole at each hook location. Thread the hooks through the center from behind and secure back side with masking tape.

Labels for cup hooks:

-s	**-es**

Duplicate the tag patterns that follow and label with these words:

cup	beach	bush
shoe	glass	box
table	match	torch
mother	bench	gas
tree	push	ash

Where do you find hippopotamuses?

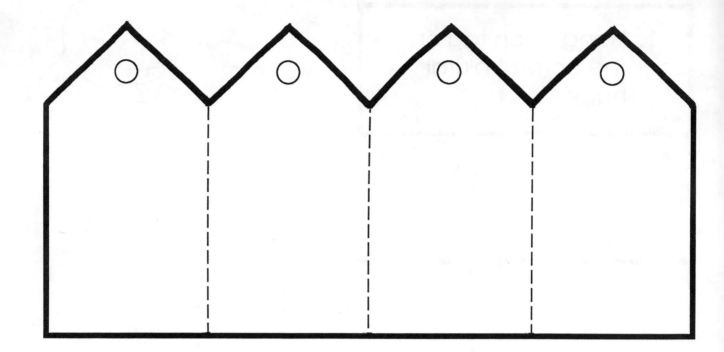

2. Checkers Game for Two Players

1. Place your checkers on the board.

2. Take turns moving from square to square.

3. To keep your square, spell the correct plural.

Note: Provide 12 checkers for each player.

Where do you find hippopotamuses?

Note: Laminate and store folded in pocket on learning center.

lake		beach		dish		witch	
	fox		watch		tax		coat
class		truck		glass		nap	
	dress		peach		pear		lunch
box		bush		sink		needle	
	crane		patch		brush		wax
fish		eraser		kiss		inch	
	bench		kitten		tent		book

Where do you find hippopotamuses?

3. Use a wipe-off crayon to cross out the plurals that are <u>incorrect</u>. Answer the questions to solve the learning center riddle.

Note: Laminate sentence card below and store in pocket on center. Provide wipe-off crayons. (Riddle answer: "Right where you left them!")

1. Mother packed six school (lunchs, lunches).
2. Are there any (boxes, boxs) left?
3. Three new (shopes, shops) have opened.
4. (Peachs, Peaches) make the best pies.
5. John needed (stitches, stitchs) on his chin.
6. Did you use the right (brushs, brushes)?
7. (Kittenes, Kittens) make good pets.
8. We bought three (records, recordes) yesterday.
9. I signed up for (classs, classes) for them.
10. We picked (bunchs, bunches) of grapes.
11. Put those (nickels, nickeles) in your pocket.
12. There were (dishes, dishs) all over the floor.
13. We bought two cake (mixs, mixes) for you.
14. Did she tell you where (glasses, glasss) are kept?
15. Joan had two (scratchs, scratches) on her leg.

WHERE DO YOU FIND HIPPOPOTAMUSES?

The word before the plural of brush: _____

The word before the plural of glass: _____

The second word after the plural of mix: _____

The word after the plural of box: _____

The second word after the plural of class: _____!

Where do you find hippopotamuses?

4. Draw the correct shape around each word to show its plural.

s =

es =

Note: Duplicate copies of the drawing sheet below and store in a pocket on the learning center.

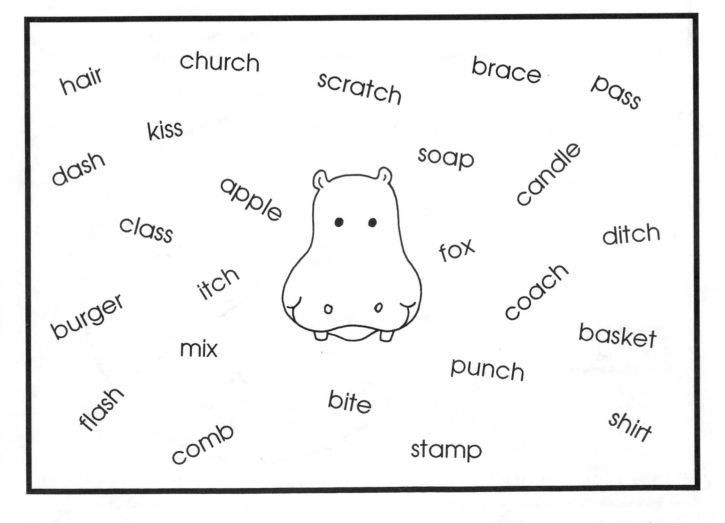

hair

church

scratch

brace

pass

kiss

soap

dash

candle

apple

class

ditch

itch

fox

burger

coach

basket

mix

punch

flash

bite

shirt

comb

stamp

Where do you find hippopotamuses?

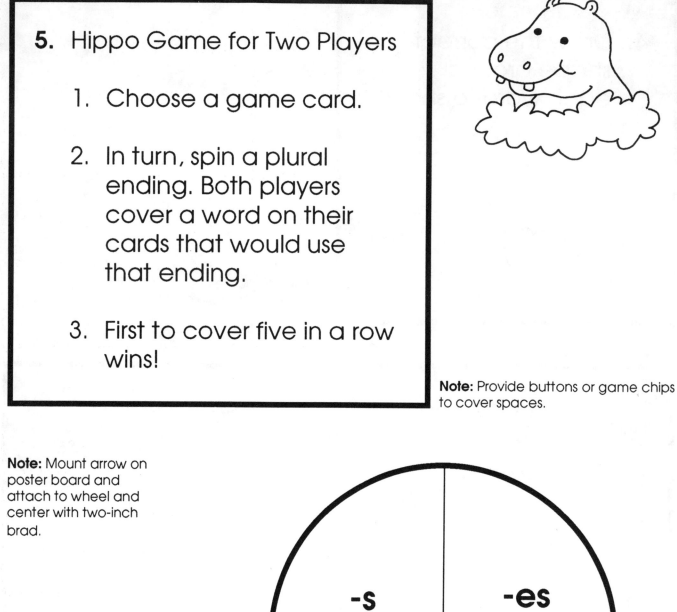

5. Hippo Game for Two Players

1. Choose a game card.

2. In turn, spin a plural ending. Both players cover a word on their cards that would use that ending.

3. First to cover five in a row wins!

Note: Provide buttons or game chips to cover spaces.

Note: Mount arrow on poster board and attach to wheel and center with two-inch brad.

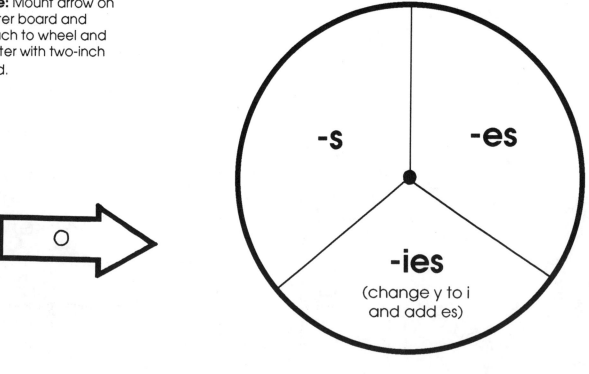

-s

-es

-ies
(change y to i
and add es)

Where do you find hippopotamuses?

Note: Store game cards in pocket on learning center.

pony	crayon	squash	flag	glass
box	vest	lady	match	bowl
city	pencil		berry	peach
army	church	corn	jet	spy
duty	bug	kiss	family	ditch
beach	lamp	canary	rose	baby
ring	poppy	lunch	hair	match
brush	chair		kitty	party
sky	witch	belt	punch	sheet
fox	bunny	track	hobby	class

Where do you find hippopotamuses?

jelly	banana	bench	country	trail
stitch	pocket	cherry	bill	patch
push	bus		puppy	wheel
game	penny	inch	box	factory
city	show	church	mystery	crutch
inch	family	glass	pony	church
brush	match	party	fox	peach
poppy	lunch		light	egg
bottle	tub	sky	bird	country
berry	skate	bunch	fairy	bull

Where does an elephant sit at the movies?

Possessives, Contractions

Where does an elephant sit at the movies?

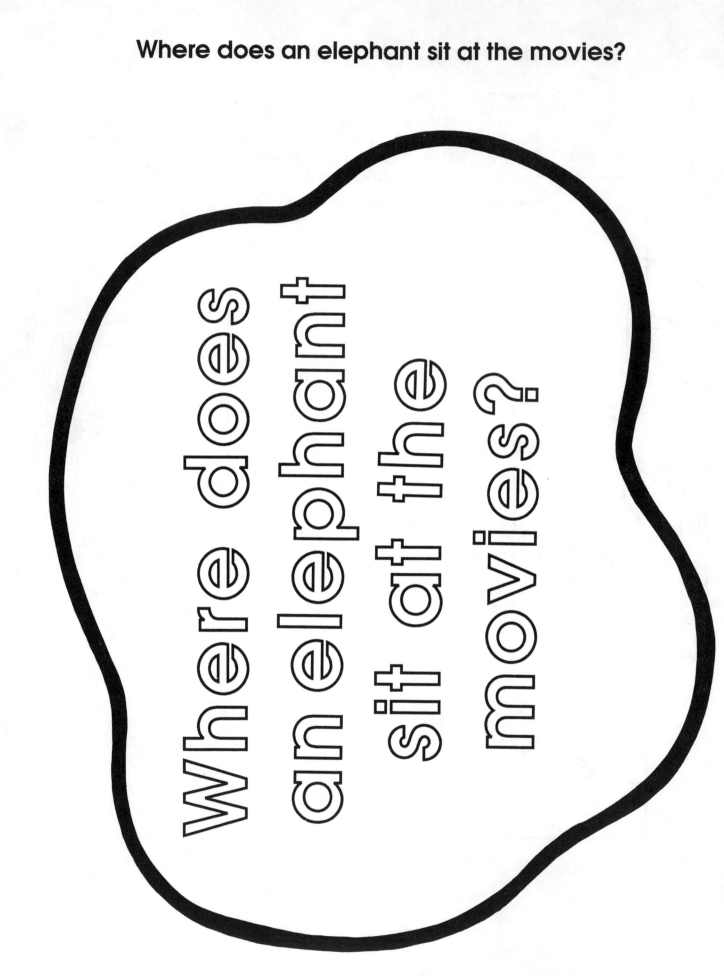

Where does an elephant sit at the movies?

 Riddles & Rhymes

Where does an elephant sit at the movies?

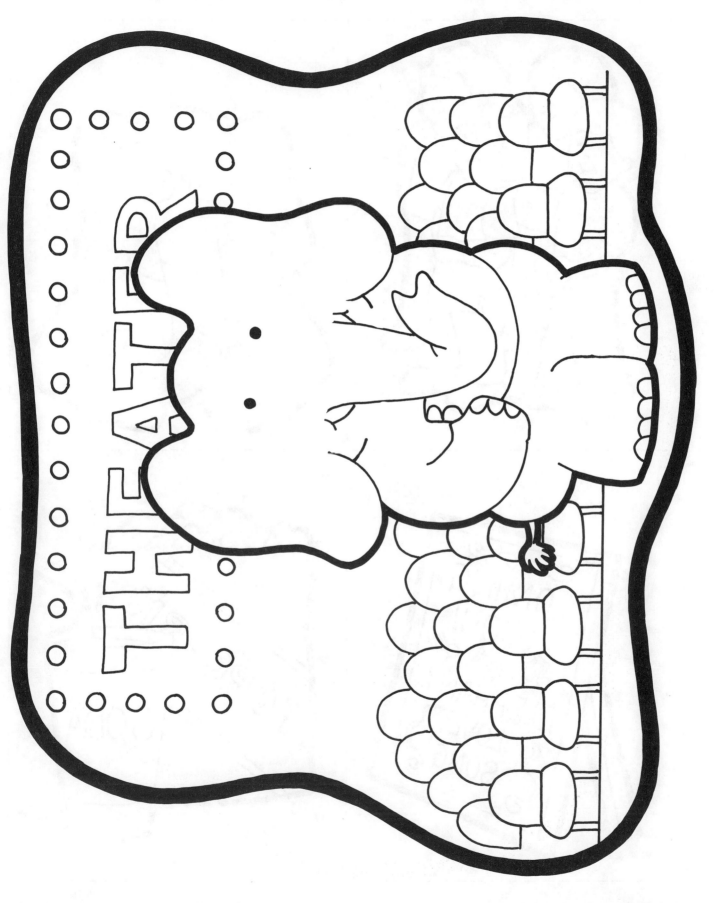

Where does an elephant sit at the movies?

COMING SOON!

ELEPHANT LOVE SONG

POPCORN

SODA

Where does an elephant sit at the movies?

Popcorn

1. Match the cards.
   Flip over to check.

Note: Code backs of correct cards with star or colored dot. Store cards in pocket on center.

Correct:

the hat belonging to the boy	the boys hat	the boys' hat	the boy's hat
the books belonging to the girls	the girls book's	the girl's books	the girls' books
the dogs belonging to Adam	Adams dog's	Adams' dogs	Adam's dogs
the recipes belonging to Grandmother	Grandmothers recipe's	Grandmothers' recipes	Grandmother's recipes

Where does an elephant sit at the movies?

Correct:

the cars belonging to the teachers	the teacher's cars	the teachers car's	the teachers' cars
the poem written by the class	the classes poem	the class' poem	the class's poem
the party given for the children	the childrens party	the childrens' party	the children's party
the tires for the buses	the buses tire's	the buses's tires	the buses' tires
the glasses belonging to Jill	Jills glasses'	Jills' glasses	Jill's glasses

Where does an elephant sit at the movies?

2. Find the missing letters from these contractions and cover them with a chip. The remaining letters will answer the learning center riddle.

Note: Use with contraction list that follows. Provide game chips or dry beans to cover letters. Store letter grid in pocket on learning center. (Riddle answer: "Anywhere he wants to!")

a	o	w	i	n	y
o	w	h	h	a	e
r	a	e	u	h	e
w	i	w	a	a	n
t	w	o	u	l	s
h	a	t	a	o	o

Where does an elephant sit at the movies?

Contractions
1. wouldn't
2. you'll
3. aren't
4. you've
5. we're
6. let's
7. she'll
8. I'm
9. he'd
10. they've
11. you're
12. doesn't

3. Stick on the missing apostrophes. You should find 9 possessives and 11 contractions.

Note: Use with story card that follows. Laminate story card and provide sticky-dot apostrophes. Store in pocket on learning center.

Where does an elephant sit at the movies?

Jumbos dad wanted to go to the movies.

"Whats playing?" Jumbo asked.

"I dont know. Lets see todays paper," said Dad. "Heres a good one, Draculas Revenge. Itll make Mothers ears flap!"

Jumbos mother was busy in the kitchen.

"Mother, lets go!" Jumbo called.

"Ill be there in a minute," she answered.

Mrs. Fizz grabbed her familys favorite snacks —the childrens cookies, the babies crackers, and Mr. Fizzs chips.

"Arent you ready? Its time to go!" called Mr. Fizz.

"Dont rush me," she said. "An elephant doesnt go anywhere without packing her trunk."

Where does an elephant sit at the movies?

4. Decide if the apostrophe makes a contraction or a possessive. Punch contraction or possessive.

Note: Tie your hole punch to the center with a string. Duplicate punch strips and store in pocket on learning center. Activity may also be completed by coloring in circles.

	Contraction OR Possessive	
○	he can't	○
○	David's jacket	○
○	the sisters' dolls	○
○	she's going	○
○	we're late	○
○	John's mother	○
○	they'll whisper	○
○	what's happening	○
○	ladies' hats	○
○	Susan's room	○
○	here's a book	○
○	aren't they	○
○	he's leaving	○
○	children's shoes	○
○	I'm ready	○

Where does an elephant sit at the movies?

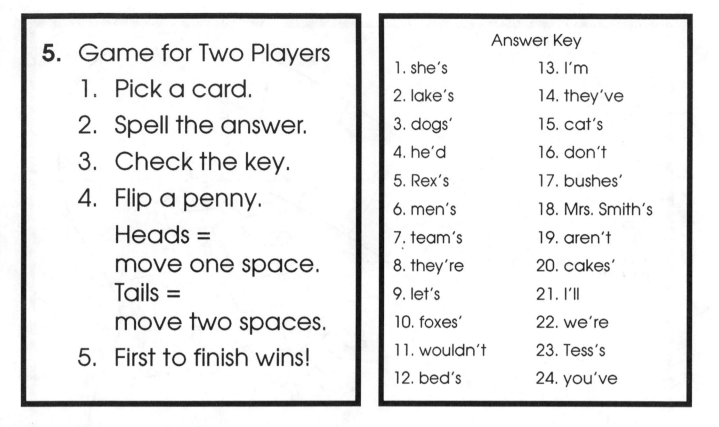

5. Game for Two Players

1. Pick a card.
2. Spell the answer.
3. Check the key.
4. Flip a penny.
   Heads =
   move one space.
   Tails =
   move two spaces.
5. First to finish wins!

Answer Key

1. she's	13. I'm
2. lake's	14. they've
3. dogs'	15. cat's
4. he'd	16. don't
5. Rex's	17. bushes'
6. men's	18. Mrs. Smith's
7. team's	19. aren't
8. they're	20. cakes'
9. let's	21. I'll
10. foxes'	22. we're
11. wouldn't	23. Tess's
12. bed's	24. you've

Note: Label 24 game cards as indicated below and store in pocket with game board that follows.

1. contraction for she is
2. belonging to the lake
3. belonging to the dogs
4. contraction for he would
5. belonging to Rex
6. belonging to the men
7. belonging to the team
8. contraction for they are
9. contraction for let us
10. belonging to the foxes
11. contraction for would not
12. belonging to the bed
13. contraction for I am
14. contraction for they have
15. belonging to the cat
16. contraction for do not
17. belonging to the bushes
18. belonging to Mrs. Smith
19. contraction for are not
20. belonging to the cakes
21. contraction for I will
22. contraction for we are
23. belonging to Tess
24. contraction for you have

Where does an elephant sit at the movies?

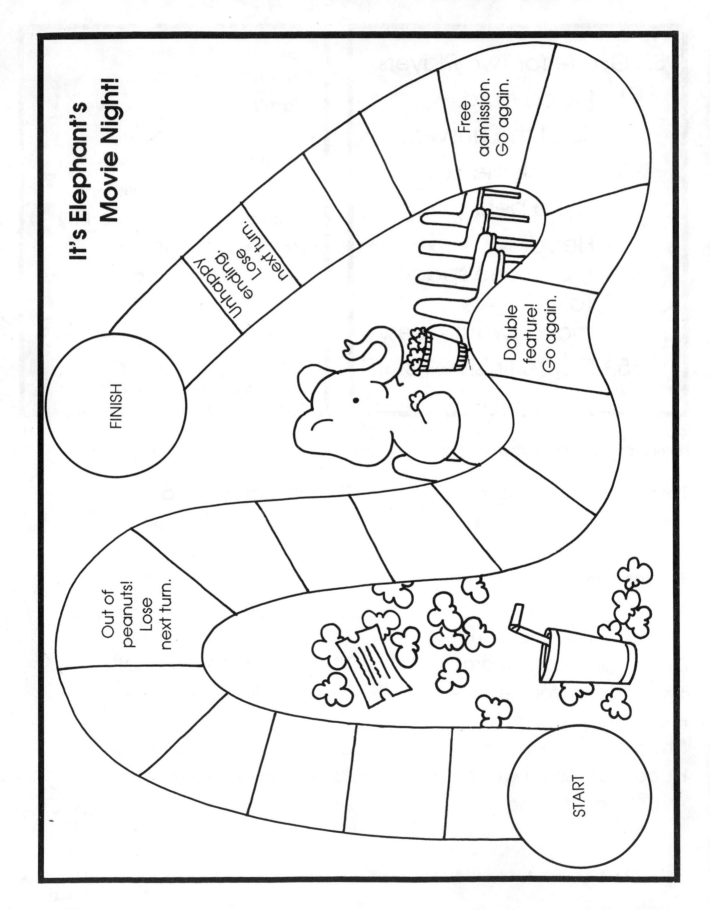

It's Elephant's Movie Night!

FINISH

Unhappy ending. Lose next turn.

Free admission. Go again.

Double feature! Go again.

Out of peanuts! Lose next turn.

START

Riddles & Rhymes